Saving Babies

The Incredible Story of a Woman Who Heard
God's Voice and a Home Called SOLVE

By Judith Berg Scott

the Peppertree Press
Sarasota, Florida

Copyright © Judith Berg Scott, 2014

All rights reserved. Published by the Peppertree Press, LLC.
the Peppertree Press and associated logos are trademarks of
the Peppertree Press, LLC.

No part of this publication may be reproduced, stored in a retrieval system, transmitted in any form or by any means, electronic, mechanical, photocopying, recording, or otherwise, without prior written permission of the publisher and author/illustrator.
Graphic design by Rebecca Barbier.

For information regarding permission,
call 941-922-2662 or contact us at our website:
www.peppertreepublishing.com or write to:
the Peppertree Press, LLC.
Attention: Publisher
1269 First Street, Suite 7
Sarasota, Florida 34236

ISBN: 978-1-61493-239-0

Library of Congress Number: 2014902294

Printed in the U.S.A.

Printed March 2014

Dedication

This book is lovingly dedicated to

Jeffrey James, Madeline Nicole, and Alexis Cara

my precious grandchildren,

with gratitude to God for the gift of your lives

Prayer of an Expectant Mother

O Almighty God, in Your wisdom You have entrusted to me a soul to be born for your honor and glory. It is a great responsibility, O Heavenly Father. I am proud and a little afraid, but I trust in Your fatherly goodness and the intercession of Your own mother, Mary, who knew all the hopes and fears of one who expects a child. Give me courage and fortitude when I need it, dear God. When the time fore-ordained by Thy wisdom shall arrive, O my God, grant me strength for a happy delivery. Let my child be born strong and healthy and filled with heavenly grace. Holy Mary, mother of Jesus, pray for me and the child to come. Amen

Prayer in card given to SOLVE clients

Found in Helen's Scrapbook

Table of Contents

	Prayer of an Expectant Mother	5
	Foreword	7
1	They're Killing My Babies	13
2	Waiting for Roland	16
3	Getting Started	20
4	Donna	24
5	Calling for Help	28
6	SOLVE Opens a Maternity Home	34
7	The Birth of the SOLVE Center	39
8	Running the SOLVE Center	45
9	A Fresh Start with Sister Gloria	50
10	God Sends the Right Person	55
11	Living at SOLVE: A warm, good place to be	59
12	Miss Donna, Come Quick!	64
13	The Girl on the Bicycle	67
14	We Wanted a House – God Gave us a Mansion	71
15	A Father's Story	78
16	A Wild Ride	82
17	Peggy	85
18	Enlarge the Place of your Tent	89
19	We Know God Brought Her to Us	96
20	The Story of the Little Breakfast Meeting	99
21	The World You Don't See	104
22	Glitz, Galas and the Quarterback's Mom	108
23	Forever Grateful	112
24	Saying Goodbye	118
25	Still, By His Grace	124
	Acknowledgements	126
	Photo Gallery	129

Foreword

WE HAD ARRANGED THE APPOINTMENT FOR 2 P.M. As I pushed the doorbell at 1:55, I knew she would be waiting, ready to tell her story. Comfortably attired in a red and white striped sweater set on this chilly day, the 84-year-old lady who answered the door smiled and graciously welcomed me into the modest home where she had lived for more than half a century.

She was slight and fragile of body with a slow, careful step, and it was hard to envision her as the feisty activist who answered God's call to save lives and change hearts so long ago. Yet that is exactly who Helen Cadoret was, and she had the thick scrapbook, carefully preserved for more than three decades to prove it. She would let me take it home this day, perhaps sensing the time had come to hand over the memories to the next generation for safe keeping. Settling down on her upholstered living room sofa, we opened it to the beginning.

Turning its yellowing pages, the history of SOLVE Maternity Homes unfolded before us through the news clippings, photos, and hand written notes that Helen had so meticulously clipped and pasted. "New group enters abortion issue." "Pregnant women in trouble find help in organization of angels." It was as carefully arranged as a baby album, each memory safely tucked inside to record the growth and development not of an infant, but of a ministry birthed to help countless babies and their mothers.

Looking at the elderly woman beside me, I wanted to know how she had done it — what had prompted her to change the course of her life and jump wholeheartedly and bravely into a mission to save babies? Tell me the story, I asked her, knowing she was ready to do just that. Gathering herself with the air of someone passing on something sacred, as indeed a lifetime's memories are, Helen remembered back to before she was even a mother herself, back to the days when she was a young girl with her whole life ahead of her. She was in love, but the world was at war.

It was 1944 and the teenaged Helen Anne Hoffman of Richmond, Virginia was engaged to the tall, handsome soldier, Roland Cadoret, five years older. "My parents wouldn't let me marry Roland before he went overseas," she confided, although that's what many other young women were doing at the time. They married when he returned after spending one year in a prisoner of war camp in Germany. "Patton liberated them," Helen said, then paused. "You know Patton?" she prompted, unsure if her younger visitor recognized the illustrious World War II general's name which she had spoken with such reverence.

She recalled what happened so many years before in the war that defined her generation. "The Russians were coming from one direction and Patton from the other — it really was a race," she said, as they tried to save the prisoners before they starved to death in the P.O.W. camps or were shot by their German captors at Hitler's command in the final days of the war. Patton ensured that her soldier was on the side of victory, living to marry the woman who would not only bear his children but rescue thousands of children in a similar race against death.

Helen had recently encountered one of those children, now a grown man 30 years old, in the aisle of a nearby grocery store. Despite the passage of so many years, his story still lingered in her heart. Remembering the frantic phone call from a woman she had never met, Helen leaned closer as she repeated what the woman had said: "She told me, 'My daughter is pregnant and considering an abortion. What can I do?'" Helen learned the daughter's boyfriend wasn't ready for a baby but through the emotional support of her mother and Helen, the girl chose not to have an abortion and gave birth to a boy. "They wound up keeping the baby and getting married," she said, smiling at the memory. The mother and daughter stayed in touch with her over the years, sharing the joy and milestones of his growing up years with the woman who had saved his life. Not until he was much older did his mother explain to him why she was so fond of "Miss Helen."

This is the story of SOLVE Maternity Homes, founded by Helen Cadoret with her husband, Roland and aided by so many dedicated volunteers to help mothers save their babies from abortion because God asked Helen to do it. It is a story of his unending faithfulness and the miracles that can happen when a person says yes to the Lord.

Not just the yes that Helen gave, but the thousands of girls and young women who came to SOLVE because they said yes to life. This is their story, too.

Chapter One

"They're Killing My Babies"

LIKE SO MANY THINGS THAT CHANGE A PERSON'S LIFE forever, it happened in church.

The year was 1976 and because of the infamous Roe v. Wade case in the United States Supreme Court three years before, abortion was now legal in America. Christians formed Respect Life groups and wrote letters to their elected officials to undo the repercussions of the court's decision. And they prayed.

Determined to do something about which she felt was a terrible wrong, 51-year-old housewife Helen Cadoret began protesting at an abortion clinic in Sarasota, Florida along with other members of the local Right to Life organization, carrying signs and praying. She hoped her presence would convince some of the girls to have their babies instead of an abortion. "When she first got started she sent me a news clipping with a picture of her picketing an abortion facility," said her oldest daughter Carollyn. "I couldn't believe it." Carollyn marveled at the boldness of her mother. "At that time, the only protesters I had heard of were war protesters. My mother sure stood up for what she believed in."

But Helen yearned to do more. As she watched young girls slowly entering the building and saw some actually being pushed into the clinic by boyfriends, she became angry, realizing that many of them really did not want to end their baby's life. But what could she do? There had to be a way for women to decide not to have an abortion, no matter what their boyfriends might say. Frustrated that she could not do more than call attention to the problem, Helen wished she could make a real difference. She just wasn't sure how to go about it.

One extraordinary evening, Helen walked into St. Joseph's Catholic Church and sat down to watch a presentation on abortion, seeing pictures of the procedure for the first time. She would never forget what she saw. "I could hardly look at those pictures," she said. In the midst of her revulsion and dismay, she heard a voice: "Helen, do something. They're killing my babies." That it came from God was never doubted by Helen, nor was the message. She understood that God was calling her in a special way to do something, and although she didn't know exactly what, it didn't matter. God would eventually reveal the answer.

She continued picketing and praying at the abortion center until one day she witnessed a scene that made it clear what she needed to do. "A guy pulled up on a motorcycle with a young girl on the back," she said, the details of what happened that day forever etched in her memory. "He just dumped her off and said, 'I'll be back when it's over.' She sat down on the curb and began to cry and I went over and put my arm around her. 'You don't have to do this, you know,' I told her. 'We can help you. I'll help you.'" Through her tears, the girl looked at Helen and said, "Well, what are you going to do for me?" At that moment, Helen knew how to answer God's call to "save my babies."

When her husband came home from work that night, Helen announced that she was starting a crisis pregnancy center. Shocked, Roland looked at her and said, "You're going to do what?" He had expected dinner, not a dramatic announcement that would turn their world upside down. Yet, believing that God had called her and being a war hero who knew plenty about fighting the good fight, Roland encouraged his wife, remaining her loyal partner in marriage and this new mission until the end of his life.

With her daughters grown and out of the nest, Helen Cadoret was ready to give hope and an alternative to abortion to girls and young women. She may have been an ordinary housewife, married 31 years and expected to start slowing down, but she was just getting started. Empowered by the Holy Spirit, Helen was transformed into a bold warrior for God, ready to do the will of him whom she loved and trusted with all of her heart. That trust would carry her forward to save lives, just as it had sustained her so many years before in a very dark hour.

Chapter Two

Waiting for Roland

ALL OF AMERICA WAS WAITING FOR HER SOLDIERS TO come home as World War II continued into 1945, praying and trusting God to bring them back soon. Helen was among them, but her calm demeanor amazed her friends who wondered why she wasn't more concerned. They knew she could hardly wait to marry Roland, the handsome soldier of French descent who was unfortunately a prisoner of war.

They met while he was playing trumpet at a USO-sponsored dance before he went overseas to the war. Roland loved music – especially Big Band swing – and Helen had discovered the night they met that he liked to dance, too. With a great sense of humor and a twinkle in his eye, he had captured her heart long before he was captured by Hitler's forces.

He traded his trumpet for a B-17 in the war, flying many successful missions for the Army Air Corps until he was shot down over enemy lines just eight days after surviving the D-Day invasion. Interrogated at a Gulag in Brussels, he was then transferred to the Stalag Luft III prison camp, 100 miles southeast of Berlin in what is today Poland. It was one of six operated by the German Luftwaffe for American and British airmen and the site of the infamous "Great Escape" that took place shortly before Roland's arrival. All but three of the 76 prisoners who had escaped through elaborate tunnels were recaptured; 50 were executed as punishment.

Helen had recently lost her father in an automobile accident and the thought that she might also lose Roland had given the teenager much heartache. But lately, she had been enveloped in a feeling of peace and confidence, for she had heard a wonderful message clearly in her heart answering her deepest prayers: "Helen, he's coming home." She believed what she heard and never told anyone why her worrying had stopped — she had been given a calm reassurance that Roland really would return to her. Trusting in the Giver of that message, Helen prayerfully waited. "I knew he was coming home," she confided many years later. "My friends didn't understand how I could be so sure. But I just knew." Pausing, she added quietly, "That's the first time I've told that story."

But things would get much worse for Roland before he could finally come home to Helen. On January 27, 1945 Hitler ordered the camp's evacuation to prevent the oncoming Russians from liberating the prisoners, who numbered more than 10,000. Given just 30 minutes to gather food and extra clothing, they began marching at midnight, trudging through the bitterly cold darkness as a blizzard swirled around them. Some did not make it.

They finally stopped, resting for 30 hours in a tile factory before marching another 15 miles to Spremberg where they were crammed into boxcars for a tortuous three day journey to Stalag VIIA outside of Moosburg in southern Germany. Many years later, Roland said the boxcars were even worse than the marching. "We had no water, no sanitation facilities. It was awful."

It was awful, too, when they arrived at Stalag VIIA — a small town of 80,000 wretched prisoners of every nationality desperately praying for an Allied victory. Soon the food ran out and the men were starving. As the Allies drew closer and the war neared its end, Hitler ordered that all prisoners be shot, but this was not carried out because the commandants knew they would be executed for the crime.

The 14th Armored Division of General George Patton's 3rd Army crashed through the gates to set the men free on April 29, 1945. The illustrious General himself arrived two days later. Roland never forgot the piece of bread one of the American soldiers gave him, savoring it like manna from heaven. "It tasted like cake to me," he remembered. Three months later he was sharing wedding cake with the girl who never doubted that happy day would come.

The newlyweds moved to his hometown of Woonsacket, Rhode Island where his father owned a jewelry store in the French speaking section of the town. Life was wonderful as Roland worked in the store and they were blessed with first one, then another baby girl, until the terrible flood of August 1955 when the Horseshoe Dam broke. With eight feet of water in the store and diamonds and jewels littered in the mud, the catastrophe gave them a good reason to flee the snow and cold. Figuring his father needed one less employee to pay as he rebuilt the store, Roland told Helen, "Why don't we go south?" They packed up Carollyn and Jo-Anne, and off they went, following Roland's dream of living in the sunshine.

They made it as far as Atlanta. Because he had been in the Air Force, Roland landed a job as an air traffic controller but after two years of the nerve wracking job— not made any easier by his night shift hours — he decided to pursue his goal of coming to the west coast of Florida. He answered an ad to manage a jewelry store in Tampa. A couple of years later when the store wanted to send him north, he instead accepted a position with another jewelry business in Bradenton, just south of Tampa on the Gulf of Mexico.

They settled in a newer cul-de-sac with other young families within walking distance of St. Joseph Catholic Church and School, around which their lives revolved for the next few decades. Weary of the frequent packing and unpacking, Helen adamantly declared to her husband, "I'm not moving anymore."

And she didn't. In 2010, the Cadorets celebrated their 65th wedding anniversary in the house, crediting their long marriage to their deep abiding faith in God as well as a sense of humor and many wonderful friends – all of which would serve them very well in the assignment God had given Helen.

Chapter Three

Getting Started

"Before I formed you in the womb I knew you, and before you were born I consecrated you."

Jeremiah 1:5

HELEN WAS READY AND WILLING TO DO GOD'S WILL, BUT how exactly was she supposed to get started? Like many Catholics with an idea, she gathered her courage and went straight to her pastor. Appointed to lead St. Joseph's Parish just the year before, Rev. Edward Moretti was a former Vietnam War chaplain who rarely talked about his experiences, saying only "I was there to serve the men, to be with them when they needed me, and to serve Mass for them in the field." He knew a thing or two about saving lives. Impressed by his parishioner with the bold plan to help women in unplanned pregnancies, he promptly wrote a personal check for $500, promising free office space, too. Such began Helen's lifelong talent for successfully asking for exactly what the organization needed — and getting it.

She did some research and found a ministry called S.O.L.V.E. in neighboring St. Petersburg and Tampa providing the kind of services she wanted to offer. It was sponsored by the Catholic Diocese of St. Petersburg, which then included Bradenton.

Although Helen's organization would be independent and not officially part of the Church – nor part of the other S.O.L.V.E. — she hoped to copy what they were doing to encourage women in unplanned pregnancies: giving maternity clothes, baby items and medical referrals, providing counseling and perhaps most importantly, offering kindness and compassion when they came for help. She knew personal contact was crucial in preventing abortion; the girl on the motorcycle had taught her that with her desperate plea, "What are you going to do to help me?"

Now that she had money, an office and a model of what was being done elsewhere, Helen was prepared to answer that question. She got right to work, rallying her friends and fellow parishioners to help out. The unwieldy acronym — Save Our Lives, Volunteer Everyway— came with the name, and people surely did; they volunteered by the dozens in whatever capacity was needed, encouraged that they now had a constructive way to do something about their belief in the sanctity of life. Many required little prodding. Women like Helen, with children grown, they were active in the Respect Life group and the St. Joseph Women's Guild and wanted to save babies. Some of their husbands joined them.

Roland was still employed full time but he quickly became his wife's biggest helper. He had left the jewelry business to work in the advertising department of The St. Petersburg Times newspaper — a job that gave him experience in putting together a monthly newsletter for SOLVE, just like he did for the local P.O.W. group. He and his wife — whose determination could sometimes be interpreted as brusque — balanced each other, benefitting not only their marriage but the organization they were busily founding. If Helen was serious, Roland had a perpetual smile and often a practical joke, but he was equally committed to the work they were doing.

SOLVE was born a week after America celebrated its Bicentennial with a nationally televised fireworks display in Washington, not far from where the Supreme Court had given its historic decision. The name Helen chose, Manasota S.O.L.V.E. Inc., reflected her desire to help women in both Manatee and neighboring Sarasota counties. Initially, she envisioned an office and outreach program. A maternity home? The idea never even crossed her mind.

Helen knew that the Catholic churches would be her natural supporters. The Church had spoken out strongly against Roe vs. Wade, proclaiming the sanctity of human life with vigor and certitude as it had since the first century, acknowledging that the right to life comes not from society, or a person, but from God alone.

> "Human life is sacred because from its beginning it involves the creative action of God and it remains forever in a special relationship with the Creator, who is its sole end. God alone is the Lord of life from its beginning until its end: no one can under any circumstance claim for himself the right directly to destroy an innocent human being."
>
> (Catechism of the Catholic Church, #2258)

And so one by one, Helen visited the 11 Catholic pastors in the area who were very glad to hear about her calling to save babies. She enlisted the help of their Respect Life groups, put notices in their church bulletins and held bake sales and bazaars to raise funds. Many loyal volunteers and donors were recruited from these churches and SOLVE took off quickly with so much Catholic support.

But Helen wasn't satisfied, for God had given her a much bigger vision. She wanted SOLVE to be ecumenical, an organization made up of Catholics and other Christians, too, and she bravely reached out to Protestant pastors for help. She wasn't afraid to approach people of other faiths who shared her pro-life passion, knowing in the end it was about saving babies, and to do that, Catholics and Protestants would have to work together.

It was a rather bold vision for the time for two main reasons. First, there were misunderstandings between faiths, especially in the southern "Bible Belt," of which Florida was certainly a part. Catholics and Protestants didn't usually worship together or work together on matters pertaining to faith. In fact, Catholics moving to Florida from more heavily Catholic parts of the country often were surprised to find themselves questioned about their beliefs as if they were less than fully Christian.

Additionally, not all agreed with the Catholic theology that a woman does not have a right to end her baby's life. Some churches and pastors had been ambivalent of the Roe v. Wade decision, believing that abortion was ultimately a matter of individual conscience. Few stood up as vehemently as the Catholic Church in protesting the court's decision and instructing their parishioners about the right to life. However, the Synod of the Christian Reformed Church took a "firm stand" against abortion in 1972, affirming the unique value of all human life from conception to the point of death.

As the years passed and Catholics continued their pro-life efforts, other Christians joined in, uniting in support of the unborn and opening dialogue and cooperation not only in Bradenton, but across the nation. "We must give credit to our Catholic friends for the wonderful job they have done. Many lives have been saved through their efforts," wrote the Rev. Bob Ritsema of Bradenton Christian Reformed Church in his Pastor's Corner three years after SOLVE was founded, encouraging his parishioners to help the organization. "Are you willing to put your beliefs into action?" he wrote. God was bringing the Body of Christ together for a specific purpose: saving babies, a trend that would continue to grow throughout the decades. He accomplished this at SOLVE right from the beginning through the openness of Helen and a beautiful young mother she would soon meet, a woman equally called by God.

Chapter Four

Donna

DONNA JEAN DEVRIES HOEKSEMA OF GRAND RAPIDS, Michigan was prepared by God from the time she was a little girl to lead SOLVE Maternity Homes into the 21st century. As surely as he called Helen to save babies, he called Donna to work right alongside her in a partnership that would save babies and help women for more than three decades.

Brought up in the Christian Reformed Church by a loving family only a generation removed from the Netherlands, Donna married her high school sweetheart when she was just 19 years old; it was all she could do to wait that long. Alvin Jack Hoeksema was 20, her first and only boyfriend. Like Donna, he was tall; his dark rugged handsomeness a contrast to her blond all-American looks that attracted appreciative glances wherever the six-foot tall beauty went.

The couple had started dating three years before and quickly fell in love. Their faith - and Donna's father – kept them pure. "My dad had me scared to even think about getting into the back seat," Donna remembers with a smile. "And I know he probably scared Al, too. There was no way we were going to do anything." Like many dads of his time, Mr. DeVries waited at the front door for his daughter to get home from her dates with Al, right up to the night before they got married in 1970. "Dad, you don't have to wait up for me tonight," Donna jokingly told him on her wedding day.

While Donna was outgoing, with a friendly, easy smile and sparkling eyes, Al was quieter, more reflective. Together they were determined to change the world for Jesus, who was the cornerstone of their lives and their marriage. They especially wanted other young people to know the peace and joy of Christ that they had found and during Al's break from Calvin College they went to Mexico for a summer of missionary work. It was rough and primitive — Donna remembers sleeping in hammocks — but they were so in love with each other and the Lord that they hardly noticed. It was a blissful time for the young couple and they later returned for a year's stay.

Donna had naturally assumed they would raise their family in Michigan near all of their relatives, but God had a different plan.

Like so many others he had called throughout history, she would be uprooted and live far from her home. Al was recruited to teach religion at a Christian school in Bradenton, Florida shortly after their first child was born. Donna can still remember the man who came to interview her husband those many years ago. She instantly took a disliking to him, perhaps because she certainly didn't expect to leave her parents and sister, with whom she was especially close, yet this man was trying to get her husband to do just that. But Al actually wanted to come to Florida and talked his wife into accepting the job.

With her firstborn 13 months old and another on the way, Donna desperately missed her family in Michigan. She didn't know anyone in Florida and besides, everything was so different here. She had easily handled the iguanas crawling on the walls in Mexico, but cockroaches? No one had warned her about the ugly insects which frightened and repulsed her and who cared if Floridians called them Palmetto bugs? And it was so hot. The only thing that seemed to pacify little Carmen was to sit her outside with the hose and let her play in the water as sweat dripped off her unhappy mother.

Things weren't so sunny for Mrs. Hoeksema in the sunshine state and she packed her suitcase to go home — surely she could persuade Al to return to Michigan, knowing this move had been a big mistake. There was just one problem, however: Al seemed quite content. What was the matter with her husband? Looking back to that miserable time, Donna said, "God had to change my heart, but first I had to let him." She finally surrendered her unhappiness to the Lord and he soon sent two angels to comfort her.

Marla Sverdlow and Wilma Schmidt may have looked like ordinary women when they arrived at Donna's home one day to introduce themselves to their new parishioner, but in reality they were an answer to the deepest prayer of the lonely mother. Not only were the three women the very same age, but they had a lot in common and quickly bonded, helping to soothe Donna's despair at being more than a thousand miles from her relatives. They became each other's family, the women as close as sisters. "None of us had our families here in Florida," said Wilma. "We raised our children together."

About that time Donna had started to protest at the local abortion facility, praying and encouraging girls not to abort while she pushed Carmen in her stroller with one hand and balanced a "Choose Life" sign in the other. She soon learned about the new organization that was trying to give women an alternative to abortion. Finally, she thought, somebody was doing something to help.

In many ways, the statuesque, blond Donna was the opposite of Helen, a brunette half a foot shorter. One was a strong Catholic, the other, a devoted member of Pastor Ritsema's Christian Reformed Church. Yet in one very important way, the young mom just starting her family and the mature woman who had already raised her children were identical: both had a profound respect for human life and a belief that God had called them to work to prevent abortions.

They officially met during a Right to Life meeting at Donna's church in 1976. "Within minutes I discovered she was one passionate woman of extraordinary faith and courage," said Donna. Helen quickly made a beeline to Donna, whom she had noticed previously while picketing, looked up at the younger woman who towered over her and blurted out, "Are you a Protestant?" Flustered, Donna didn't know what to make of the abrupt and unusual question. She called herself a Christian and didn't use the word Protestant, and besides, why had she asked that? Helen explained her vision of an ecumenical organization made up of the entire Body of Christ, thereby weaving a common thread within the community to support life. She already had the Catholics; now she needed the Protestants. Was that Donna?

"She had me," said Donna, understanding immediately what Helen was trying to do. Helen had found her Protestant. Donna appreciated what Helen and the Catholic churches were doing and liked the idea of working together. Theirs would be a mutual relationship of love and respect, a partnership to help women and save babies spanning thirty five years, ending only when Donna stood to give the eulogy at Helen's funeral in the church where it all began.

These two dynamic women of faith would combine forces to lead SOLVE under God's direction, experiencing his provision and miracles in ways they could hardly have imagined in that Bicentennial summer.

Chapter Five

Calling for Help

"Hi, I'm pregnant....I don't know what to do!" Please help me."

Helen and her volunteer crew were preparing to officially open the SOLVE office for business that sizzling July day in 1976 when a young girl picked up the phone and dialed the number she had seen in the classifieds. Her name was Marlene. Just 16 years old, she was SOLVE's very first client.

Little did Marlene know that she was about to make history. She only knew that she needed a place to stay for the remainder of her pregnancy and the advertisement had given her some hope. She was not disappointed. SOLVE paid rent on a small apartment for five weeks until she delivered a boy on September 1. SOLVE's first baby had been born!

The second SOLVE baby, a girl, was born on September 19th and another one two days later. While these mothers had chosen life for their babies before contacting SOLVE, they nevertheless reached out to the new organization for help. They had seen the small ad running daily in the newspaper: "Pregnant? Thinking of abortion? Don't! We will help you 24 hrs. a day" or perhaps one of the bright yellow stickers pasted up around town with SOLVE's telephone number. Within the first three months there were 78 calls, nearly one every day.

Helen knew that a telephone "hot line" was an essential component of SOLVE's mission and so it operated 24 hours a day from the start. At night the answering machine gave out the phone number of a volunteer waiting at home, ready to wake up and serve when the call came. Brimming with enthusiasm, Helen's dedication was contagious, spilling over to the volunteers she recruited in droves, including 30 people right away taking telephone shifts. All of them were women because Helen thought the girls would prefer to talk with another female.

Many girls in an unexpected pregnancy couldn't bring themselves to confide in their families. When the phone volunteers asked the girls if they had told their parents, they often replied, "My mother would have a heart attack if I told her I am pregnant," or something similar. They were afraid, unsure of the reaction they would get from their mother and father and fearing the worst. Just having someone else to talk to about it often made the difference in saving her baby's life.

That was the case late one Friday afternoon when Donna was working in the office and a young lady walked in requesting counseling. She had already been to the abortion clinic and now she wanted Donna's advice. After an hour of listening, talking, praying and studying brochures depicting the growth of an unborn baby, she left. The following Monday morning Donna called her, asking if she would be willing to come back and talk some more. A few days later she returned and told Donna that she had decided to have her baby. When Donna asked what made her change her mind against having an abortion, she replied, "I just needed someone to tell me it was OK to have my baby."

Surprisingly, many of the calls, almost half, came from married women. Some just needed a pregnancy test or help with medical services or baby items, which the volunteers gladly provided. Others, however, were being pressured by their husbands to get an abortion, an option which had only been legal for a few years. Because of the Supreme Court's controversial ruling, married couples had choices that were previously unthinkable.

Helen and the other volunteers – who had so joyfully welcomed their own children and raised them lovingly - were always dismayed when those calls came in. They tried to help the girls encourage their husbands to welcome the babies and often were successful. Sometimes it just took a little while for the man to get used to the idea.

Most of the other callers were girls still living at home until their pregnancy was discovered, at which time many parents would make them leave unless they agreed to an abortion. "I'm nineteen years old and pregnant," began one girl. "I haven't heard from my fiancé since he was discharged from the Air Force. My parents have given me one week to move out. Can you help me?"

While families previously had sent their daughters away to a relative in another state or a maternity home elsewhere so that no one would find out, now with abortion legal, that was seen as a simpler solution for all. There was no need to make elaborate plans or pretend their daughter was "away at school" and no one would ever know. Even many Christian families felt that if it was legal, it must be OK, ignoring the tug of conscience. It took courage for girls to reject abortion when the people all around them were suggesting it, sometimes even their doctors.

They drew strength from the encouraging voices they heard on the hotline. "The most important thing we do is show the girls we really do care and give them a shoulder to lean on," Helen explained. One of those girls, now herself a grandmother thanks to SOLVE, came into the office many years later and said, "When people who don't know you love you so much and care about you and make you feel valued and important, that is life changing. My life is not perfect and I have made mistakes, but Miss Helen taught me that the important thing is to get back up, learn from them and to move on, because God has a plan for me."

Helen listened without judgment and expected all of the volunteers, who were trained extensively in what to say and how best to serve the girls, to do likewise. Her training brochure, with guidelines and rules from the original SOLVE, stated:

"Your interest in talking with these girls personally lets me know that you are a very special person; a woman with love in her heart for both mother and the unborn child. Because of this love, I know that you will treat all of your clients with warmth and compassion, being ever mindful that no matter what they have done, or not done, that for the Grace of God, it would be you seeking their help."

The brochure continued with good advice:

"Listen calmly while the girl talks. Reassure her that you personally and the SOLVE organization will be very happy to help her. Put yourself in her shoes and you'll make out beautifully. We are not here to judge….only to love."

That spirit of love, not judgment, permeated SOLVE from the beginning. Its mission was to give women an alternative to abortion, to help them make the decision to have their babies, yet never in a preaching or "holier than thou" attitude.

Helen took a lot of the calls herself. She grew to love many of the girls, some of whom considered her a substitute mother and kept in touch over the years. Even decades later, she could remember the names and faces of surprisingly many of SOLVE's clients. An extremely meticulous, detailed woman, she wrote down every call on a piece of lined paper, noting the name, the date and a detail or two in her neat Palmer penmanship: How old the client was, how far along in the pregnancy, what town she was from. Later, when a baby was born she went back and in red marker, noted the sex of the baby and date of birth.

Dorothy, the seventh caller, had been referred to SOLVE by the abortion clinic; she had apparently changed her mind about ending her pregnancy. Helen's log noted she gave birth to a girl six months later. Line by line, name by name, the log offered a glimpse into so many young lives, the few words in blue ball point pen revealing only the barest details of the heartache that brought them to pick up the telephone. Diane was a newcomer. Evelyn was on welfare. Theresa's boyfriend was in the service, and Rita needed a crib. Katherine's husband wanted the abortion, but the red word "Girl" proves a life was spared. Or, a not uncommon scenario with Deborah, the 61st caller: "Granny sez out!" Even grandmothers could only take so much.

Towards Christmas of that first year, a teenager, pregnant and newly divorced, called in desperation. She was about to be evicted. The phone volunteer convinced her to come into the office. It was a cold day yet she arrived without a sweater or even shoes, no money and even less hope. What she did have was the promise of her parents, who lived in Ohio, that she could live with them if only she could get there, as they could not afford to pay her way. The newly formed Action Committee lived up to its name, finding clothing, shoes and warm boots and purchasing an airline ticket to send her home. SOLVE had limited financial means which would have been depleted quickly if not controlled; the committee's job was to determine available aid and where best to give it.

SOLVE helped in as many ways as there were girls calling. The volunteers even found jobs for some of the mothers and helped others find the right agency if she wished to release her baby for adoption. It was incredible everything that the volunteers did for the girls, all on a shoestring budget with no paid staff, using Helen's reliable station wagon as the delivery vehicle when needed.

The SOLVE newsletter of January 1977 reported: "During our first six months of operation we have had over 150 calls, and 66 women and girls have received medical, financial, and psychological aid. Maternity and baby clothes continue to be our fastest moving items in both supply and demand. Our inventory of six cribs and mattresses is exhausted."

Helen, with the help of many faithful volunteers, had certainly answered God's call to "Do something." But none of them had any idea of the big surprise he had waiting for them just around the New Year.

Chapter Six

SOLVE
Opens a Maternity Home

A MATERNITY HOME WAS NOT PART OF HELEN'S INITIAL plan to save babies from abortion; however, as the new year of 1977 rolled around, she soon learned that God had his own plan, and he was quickly setting it in motion.

Deeply touched by the work SOLVE was doing, a couple generously donated a brand new duplex to the Diocese for the exclusive use of SOLVE. Excited by John and Margaret McGee's gift, although aware that the duplex set up might not be quite right for a maternity home, the Board of Directors nevertheless gratefully accepted it. No one involved in the young organization had ever run a maternity home. It was one thing to run an office and phone line, but a live in facility? God was literally opening a door and leading them through it; they just had to lean on him to see it to completion.

Supporters filled the new home with donated furniture and lovingly decorated it, thinking girls would quickly move in and wanting it to be as homey and cheerful as possible.

SOLVE planned to have the girls live on one side of the duplex and hire a house mother who would live on the other side; the office would also be moved on site. What they hadn't planned on was the reaction of the neighbors, who protested to the Manatee County Planning Commission. Helen and the Board of Directors were caught off guard. Although the people living in Sunny Lakes Estates said they appreciated what SOLVE was trying to do by helping pregnant girls, they did not want a maternity home in their subdivision, especially with an office. They complained that it would increase traffic and was not in keeping with normal activities in a residential area.

But that was not the only holdup to welcoming pregnant girls into the home. The Catholic Diocese, legal owners of the duplex, required that funding, personnel, and policies be in place prior to its opening, which took time to develop. SOLVE had announced the new home in January, yet it still sat empty as "Away in a Manager" played on the radio that Christmas.

No one ever said doing God's will was easy.

It appeared that a major miracle was needed and the foundress asked supporters to "storm heaven with our prayers!" Despite her keen disappointment at not being able to open the house, Helen drew encouragement from remembering the purpose of SOLVE: "I had the rewarding experience of holding a beautiful one week old baby boy who certainly would have been aborted were it not for the efforts of SOLVE volunteers," she wrote to supporters. "It is moments such as this that make all our trials and tribulations worthwhile, and I wish all of you could have been there. The joy this baby brought to his very young, but loving, parents reinforces the necessity to combat abortion on every front!"

Finally, one year after it's hoped for opening, approval was granted — although the zoning exemption to also allow the office at that site had been denied by the county. Helen had pushed hard for having the office on site. The denial, however, came with a silver lining: it accelerated plans to expand the ministry.

They soon opened a second office in Sarasota County and a bigger office in Bradenton. Virginia McCormack, whose husband, Richard, the first vice president of SOLVE, had told a reporter "Abortion is not a religious issue, it's a moral one," ran the newest office, the McCormacks attended Incarnation Catholic

Church in Sarasota after their retirement from New York. Not content to while away their remaining years in leisure, the couple quickly recruited dozens of volunteers, primarily from their parish. In just six weeks they helped 21 women. They devoted much time and effort to SOLVE from the beginning, so when they decided to move to the mountains of North Carolina a year later, they were greatly missed. God had used them to help get SOLVE up and running.

On March 30, 1978 the maternity home welcomed its first resident. It really looked like a home: every room was tastefully furnished with items given by businesses and individuals, some of whom even made draperies, cut the lawn and stocked the cupboards.

Mary Scott, who agreed to temporarily serve as the first house mother until a permanent candidate could be hired after responding to an ad in her church bulletin, was amazed at all of the interest and support. "It's because of Helen's total dedication to SOLVE," she said when interviewed by The Florida Catholic newspaper. "She knows how to ask for what is needed." Helen's practical point of view was that "If you don't ask, you don't receive. We have only to ask and our needs are met." Her faith in God and her fellow man did not let her down. She had always known this was God's ministry and that they never would have accomplished what had been done so far without his divine guidance. "SOLVE would never be where it is if God wasn't with us at every turn," she firmly stated. That's why she was not hesitant to put out a request for "some good drivers with big hearts and full gas tanks." With girls needing to visit the doctor, shop, and maybe even go to classes, her car would not be enough. She also asked for caring volunteers to teach the girls skills like sewing and even to take them on outings and perhaps offer them a part time job.

This first house remained open for a little over a year. It wasn't long, but to Yvonne, Toni, Rebecca, Anita, Mary, Dawn, Ann, Ronni, Kathy, Terri, Wendy, and Theresa, it made all the difference in the world. Their 12 babies — seven of whom were released for adoption – are now possibly raising their own families and likely unaware of the part SOLVE played in saving their life.

During that time, an unusually high percentage of SOLVE's clients expressed serious plans to terminate their pregnancies. Three came to SOLVE on the very day they were scheduled to have an abortion. "Without a doubt, these innocent unborn babies were saved through the grace of God and the availability of Manasota SOLVE," marveled Helen.

A few girls stayed at the home for a brief time while they made other arrangements; one for example, waited until she got the OK from her sister to move in with her in another state, and a 17-year-old, whose mother was pushing her to get an abortion, sadly left after a few days to do just that despite SOLVE's best efforts to save her baby. Laurie was five months pregnant and her mother had to drive her to Miami to receive this late abortion.

It was crushing when a girl chose to abort her baby after receiving help from SOLVE. Still, Helen and all of the volunteers knew they had done their best to save the baby. It was difficult to accept but they persevered, strengthened by the precious babies they were saving and the many girls and women who were experiencing God's love through their efforts. And so they carried on.

When the couple who had come from Ohio to take on the job as permanent houseparents decided not to return after their vacation, it gave the board an opportunity to re-evaluate how it was working. They temporarily closed the house while a replacement was found. It was briefly reopened, but because of numerous problems, SOLVE reluctantly closed its first maternity home permanently in April of 1980 as they tried to figure out what to do next.

It had been an astounding four years for SOLVE. Incredibly, except for the paid houseparents, it was all accomplished by volunteers. Helen had converted one of the bedrooms in her house into an office so that she could continue working when she went home, hanging a bulletin board over her desk with files and notebooks scattered around near the telephone which sat nearby. She never took a penny during her three decades of what was usually the equivalent of full time service; hers was always a labor of love.

Love transformed the life of a woman who sent this letter to SOLVE 18 years later:

> *A young girl got pregnant and when she told her boyfriend, he told her to get an abortion. She refused to do so and the boyfriend left her. She came to SOLVE and delivered a beautiful girl whom she named Angel. The woman later on married a man who loved this little girl deeply. You see he was unable to have children and my Angel became a blessed angel in our family. Angel graduated from High School this year – and P.S. she is beautiful."*

Chapter Seven

The Birth of the SOLVE Center

SOLVE HAD LEARNED TO RUN A MATERNITY HOME THE hard way – by experience. They had discovered what worked and what didn't work, and with the home now closed, the Board considered what to do next. Where was God leading them?

It was evident that having the office away from the maternity home —leaving the house mother alone while caring for a house full of pregnant girls – did not work. It was a stressful, emotional job at times; having support staff close by was essential. "I'd have to run down there every time there was a problem, which was often," said Helen. Also, the duplex set up was less than ideal and did not easily lend itself to community living, a drawback the Board had worried about from the beginning. They wanted the girls to feel part of a family, with the houseparents acting as substitute parents and mentors. Lack of convenient medical care was another big concern. Thus, the Board decided to examine more closely what worked best for similar ministries.

A thorough study was conducted by the SOLVE Center Committee, consisting of Helen and Roland, David Montgomery, Juanita Robbins and Jeanne Hofflich. Their report, as exhaustive and well written as any Fortune 500 Company's investigation, convinced the rest of the Board to sell the duplex and support what the committee called a SOLVE Center. They knew they needed a larger, centrally located building where the home and office were together, making SOLVE much easier to manage. Problems could be resolved before they had time to exacerbate and services could be more conveniently provided.

The Diocese of St. Petersburg gave approval to sell the duplex and in early 1981, SOLVE sold its first maternity home for $42,000. Now they began to search for another home. They thought they knew just what they were looking for and with a sizeable down payment, they expected to find it rather quickly.

While the hunt for a SOLVE Center continued, so did the phone calls, but now there were two offices in need of volunteers, especially every spring when Florida's "snowbirds" returned to their northern homes. Helen put notices in church bulletins and the newsletter for more people to fill their place: "Remember, experience is not necessary. You will be trained. All you need is compassion and love for the unborn." Faithfully, new volunteers always seemed to answer the call, ready to help however they could. They were people like Peggy Roberts, who despite suffering from multiple sclerosis took hot line calls in the evening from her home. The former social worker cheerfully said, "I am glad God gives me the strength to be able to serve others via the telephone," which she did for many years.

SOLVE's brochure told the girls, "Whatever is troubling you won't seem so heavy when you talk it over with a friend who wants to help."

Their questions were as different as each girl:

- How can I tell if I'm pregnant?
- How should I tell my family?
- How can I continue school?
- Where can I get medical care?
- Can I keep my baby?
- What about adoption?
- What about my baby's father?

- Will drugs hurt my baby?
- Can I lose my job if they find out I'm pregnant?
- How can I get maternity clothes?

If a volunteer didn't know the answer, she found someone who did. They also provided transportation to medical and welfare facilities, food vouchers from St. Vincent de Paul Society, baby sitting and even some housing in private homes. A few generous families welcomed girls into their homes, including the Cadorets – whose daughters learned to ask for Helen when they called because they never knew who would pick up the phone – but seldom would they take another when she left with her baby. It was just too much disruption for most families to handle. The pressure to open the SOLVE Center increased with every call.

A concerned teacher sought information for a 16-year-old student whose father was kicking her out. "Can you hide me?" asked the girl, who said her father was forcing her to get an abortion. A 23-year-old woman called after being deserted by her boyfriend and a 28-year-old woman who left her ex-husband's house was now seven months pregnant. "I'm a college freshman," began one girl. "I'm pregnant. My parents won't let me go back home while I'm showing. I don't know what to do." A rape victim, who came to Bradenton to have her baby, called for help. Embracing her with compassion, the volunteers helped her get aid and food stamps and fervently wished the SOLVE Center was already open for her.

Other kinds of calls came in, too. Girls shared the happy news that their babies had been born, grateful for the help they had been given. Occasionally, they even called to invite Helen or Donna or one of the volunteers to their wedding.

Because governmental services to indigent pregnant women were not what they are today, SOLVE also provided financial assistance in a variety of ways, including guidance through the intricate procedures of welfare agencies. Needy women often made too much money to qualify for welfare, not eligible for indigent status despite incomes that were quite low. Sometimes they just showed up at the public hospitals for delivery without any prior pre-natal care.

Some of the volunteers were retired nurses and other health professionals and social workers who were able to help quite a bit. They gave pregnant women vitamins along with nutrition counseling and encouragement, but that was the best they could do with few options in the way of medical care referrals. Through the next few years, Helen and Board member Lois Henderson fought hard to get access to pre-natal health care for the girls who came to them. "Every girl who is about to deliver can go to the emergency room of any public hospital and the hospital is obliged to deliver," Lois stated in an interview published in the newspaper about the problem. "They will send her a whopping bill afterward for both the hospital and the doctor's service and she'll pay for it, if and how she can." Some doctors did offer reduced rates to SOLVE clients.

In the fall of 1984, due to pressure not only from SOLVE but other women's organizations, both counties served by SOLVE made pre-natal care possible for their clients: The Sarasota Public Health Clinic accepted qualified girls for pre-natal services and delivery, while in Manatee County, the Samoset Clinic provided obstetric care to pregnant women with low incomes.

Meanwhile, the Board was discovering that it wasn't so easy after all to find a house that could be used for a SOLVE "Center." There were so many requirements: it had to be zoned commercial, be close to shopping, bus lines and the hospital, have four bedrooms to accommodate at least six girls and yet be within their price range. It also had to meet with the approval of the Board, which some said would be a minor miracle itself. Several times they thought they had found it, but it never seemed to be quite right.

In truth, after a while there was also the nagging temptation to simply stick with the phone line and office. Wasn't that enough? That was a great service in itself and running a maternity home was demanding. But, as the Committee's detailed report stated, "We must resist the temptation to take the easy way out. That is, eliminate our own housing facilities and all of the problems that go with it. But this would dilute our ability to provide good and immediate emergency care that could save babies. We need to be recognized by the high school girl who is on the brink of having an abortion out of desperation."

Helen added her own emphatic P.S. to the Committee's report: "As in any business, we cannot stand still. We are either going forward, or we're going backwards. We can now look back with pride at what we've accomplished since our first small office in 1976. But if we become self satisfied and lose the will to move aggressively forward towards greater heights so we can do a better job, we'll be copping out" she wrote, urging the Board to stay focused on the SOLVE Center.

After a year's search, they finally found a house on a tree-lined street in a residential downtown Bradenton neighborhood. Built in 1915 before she was even born, Helen delightedly proclaimed that the two story brick home was "perfect." In nearly move-in condition, it had six bedrooms, three baths and a large front porch typical of its era — it even had a fireplace – and was as charming as the advertisement claimed. An unattached garage could be used as the office, with plenty of room for the required parking spaces.

In July 1982, exactly six years after they began, SOLVE agreed to purchase the house for $75,000, almost nine thousand less than the asking price (and paid off the mortgage in two years). Not wanting to repeat their past mistakes, they wisely formed a plan for getting the neighbors on their side, visiting each one and handing out copies of the positive articles that had run in the newspaper about SOLVE and asking for their support. They also hired R. E. Nelson, Inc. to get the special exemption it would need as a community care facility through the bureaucratic complexities, which was approved the next month. They didn't fail to notice that the closing date — September 1 — was the same date their very first baby had been born.

In what turned out to be providential timing, the opening of the Center coincided with the 10th anniversary of Roe v. Wade on January 22, 1983. The media was filled with stories covering the decade of legal abortion, including a lengthy article about what SOLVE was doing to help girls as an alternative to abortion. An editorial in the local newspaper even asked readers for contributions of money, food and baby supplies.

The publicity helped SOLVE financially and with public support just when they needed it most. Their budget had increased dramatically now that they again had a maternity home to run and a house mother to pay. While the opening of the newest house hadn't been planned for that particular time, it was one more sign that God was looking after his dedicated little band of servants busy saving his babies.

Chapter Eight

Running the SOLVE Center

When the SOLVE Center opened for residents that January, girls found a charming home decorated as if special guests were coming to stay, right down to the pretty matching towels in the bathrooms and the original crystal chandelier gleaming brightly over the dining room table. Women from Helen's parish and other volunteers had spent hours polishing, cleaning, and decorating to create a welcoming oasis for its inhabitants. When it needed new carpet a few years later, they pulled up the old carpet to discover beautiful wood floors installed more than 70 years earlier still in excellent condition.

Helen's first task had been to hire a live-in house mother who earned a modest stipend with free room and board.

Girls moved in quickly. First came Jenny, who left home because her parents were so upset about the pregnancy that it was impossible for her to remain there. Thankfully, the maternity home had opened in time to save her baby's life; she was already three months pregnant.

Another teenager hopped on a bus in Virginia after her boyfriend took off, arriving with all of $3 left in her pocket and hopes that her family in Bradenton would help her. When they could not, she realized she was running out of options. As she sat in a coffee shop wondering what to do, she began looking through a newspaper that happened to be lying on the table. "Pregnant? Desperate? SOLVE will help you and your baby," read the ad that seemed to be written just for her. She quickly dialed the phone number, reaching Donna, who was now serving on the newly formed "House Committee."

A team of volunteers made up this committee to run the maternity home, handling everything from maintenance to decision making for issues that cropped up daily. Vicki Hilferding volunteered on the committee and like Donna, Vicki's strong pro-life beliefs fueled her passion to help save babies. However, while Donna was orderly and Biblical, Vicki was more street savvy. They made a good team, "iron shaping iron," as Donna described it, helping each other see all sides of a problem.

When Donna answered the call from the girl in the coffee shop, she wanted to discuss with Vicki what to do. Helen's motto was to never turn anybody away, however, they had to apply and be screened before being admitted and Donna was inclined to follow those rules.

But a desperate girl with nowhere to go was waiting nearby. Vicki suggested that she and Donna drive over to meet her and if she seemed "OK," they would take her in, which Donna agreed was a sensible solution. Happy to be offered a bed at SOLVE, she grew very close to the volunteers and the housemother, who helped fill the void her family's absence caused. She had already decided that she would not raise her child and released her baby for adoption. "I think that's the best thing to do for both of us."

Now that the SOLVE Center was a reality, they thanked Father Moretti for allowing them to use space at the church for seven years and moved the Bradenton office to the new site. Helen and the Board were grateful to have the house and office at one location, a primary goal of their search committee. Not only did it make SOLVE more visible in the community, it also enabled the residents to interact with the volunteers and phone counselors during office hours. Although there was not a paid counselor on staff yet, compassionate volunteers always seemed to have time to listen as a girl poured out her heart. Shoulders to cry on were plentiful and free.

Just before the maternity home opened, John Zilles came forward with a fundraising offer: he would raise poinsettias to sell in time for Christmas. The 74-year-old was a retired chemical engineer who oversaw Henry Ford's Brazilian rubber tree plantations before World War II. Well known for growing poinsettias, he had raised thousands of poinsettias — and dollars — for another organization and now wanted to do the same for SOLVE. Many of the churches ordered the plants to decorate their sanctuaries and also sold them to parishioners. That first sale netted $4,000 along with plenty of newspaper coverage, which increased to $12,000 and more publicity the second year. The local newspaper even saluted Mr. Zilles for "making a difference." Thirty years later, the poinsettia sale remains a Christmas tradition and an important budget booster.

By January of 1984 the house had been opened for one year, providing refuge for 17 young, homeless women. Fourteen babies had been born (six had been released for adoption). SOLVE was operating without any governmental help, or interference, but not for long.

In the spring of 1984, SOLVE was notified by the state of Florida that because they housed girls under the age of 18, they would have to obtain a state license as a Child Care Facility. This necessitated many renovations in order to comply with the safety requirements, including the construction of a fire escape from a second story bedroom and cutting a hole in the bedroom wall to create a door leading to it. More than one house mother over the years would rue that hidden entry into the house! A few girls had trouble following the "no boyfriends in the house" rule, it seemed.

SOLVE was licensed for the first time in July of 1984 as its eighth anniversary rolled around. Several years later they would become one of the first facilities to be licensed under the newly created category of maternity home.

Another state requirement was that they hire an administrator. Up to this point there was just one person on the payroll —- the house mother —with everything else handled by dedicated volunteers. There were offices in two counties and a 24-hour helpline as well as the maternity home, yet no one was getting paid – at least not in this life —and they were all doing an excellent job. Increasing governmental demands added to the operational costs. More funds would be needed to pay for this position, and as he always had, God continued to provide.

A dedicated volunteer began a Green Stamp Campaign to collect the once popular trading stamps grocery stores gave customers, which could be redeemed for all kinds of merchandise. Marty Young was concerned that SOLVE did not always have enough baby items to hand out to the needy women who came to the two offices for help. Sometimes she would put the name of the expectant mother on a waiting list and give her a call if the item she needed was donated or returned.

In her first year, Marty got the area Catholic churches to participate and raised more than $6,000 worth of baby cribs, swings and other necessities. Cardinal Mooney High School even allowed the students a "no uniform" day if they would bring in a book of stamps, which continued to pour in long after the campaign ended. When she kicked off her second effort, the Sarasota newspaper published a lengthy article along with a large photo of Marty and Lois Henderson surrounded by baby items, bringing in not only Green Stamps but new volunteers and financial contributions that greatly helped as SOLVE's budget grew.

God's call to "do something" was growing into a bigger and more complicated something as the years went on, yet his guidance and blessings poured over them all. Every morning when Helen woke up, she prayed, "OK, God, what are we going to do today?" And together, they figured it out.

"My thanks to all of you at SOLVE for your help and guidance when I really was down. I don't know what I would have done without you. My baby and I had a rough first year. But now I have an apartment and a job. I know the Lord is always with me. Don't ever give up the great work you are doing!"

FROM A LETTER RECEIVED IN 1985

Chapter Nine

A Fresh Start with Sister Gloria

HELEN WOKE UP ONE JULY MORNING IN 1986 AND COULD hardly believe it. SOLVE was 10 years old! How generous God had been in supplying all their needs, and then some, in the past decade. Celebrating joyfully with a Happy Birthday banquet, they honored Gertrude Cavanaugh, Lucille Culbreath, and Kathleen Murphy, three original volunteers, for their 10 years of faithful service, knowing many more had helped over the years to keep it all going.

Helen calculated that an astonishing 2,498 girls and women received services of some kind that first decade, most of whom sought help at the two offices where they could take a free pregnancy test, pick out something from the "Giving Closet," get help with medical bills or other financial needs, or be directed to other services. Among that number were 74 girls who came to live at SOLVE.

The next few years passed quickly in a blur of blessings and babies. More and more girls were calling SOLVE for help and thankfully supporters insured that SOLVE could respond. Meanwhile, volunteers kept the house in shape and Roland was called to duty for every needed repair. They stretched the budget as tight as the proverbial drum, rejoicing in the surprise financial gifts that came in as they always seemed to just in the nick of time.

By 1993, however, one problem could not be denied. The organization Helen had founded to save babies had done just that for nearly 17 amazing years, but rapid turnover in the administrator's position was stressful. Several directors came and went for a variety of reasons and there had also been too many house mothers to count. It seemed that the newsletter was always welcoming somebody or saying goodbye. "We would have to train a replacement all over again," complained Helen.

Unhappy with the turnover, Helen believed she had the solution to finding someone who would make a more permanent commitment and also run SOLVE the way she thought it should be run. She had not always agreed with everything the various directors had done over the years and some just hadn't seemed to be the right fit. But she had an idea: hire a nun! Helen thought that finding the perfect Sister would also eliminate some of the discipline problems that had cropped up with society's changes since 1976, perhaps remembering her own youth when no one questioned or challenged Sister. She was elated when Sister Gloria Hillman answered an ad for the job in January of 1994 and remained until the end of the decade.

Wearing street clothes instead of a nun's habit, Sister Gloria brought a fresh start after that stressful period. Her background in counseling, psychology and teaching was quickly put to use as the Dominican Sister of Hope tried to give exactly that to the residents. She understood that some of the girls brought more than a suitcase; many carried emotional and psychological baggage, too. She tried to find something in each resident to praise and challenged them to find positive traits in each other, too.

At the time, SOLVE was one of the few maternity homes where a girl could live if she was planning to keep her baby. Sister Gloria, however, did her best to increase adoptions and strongly encouraged the girls to consider it, knowing how difficult it would be for them as single mothers. One of the young ladies who did heed Sister Gloria's advice to release her baby was Sara (not her real name). A rebellious teenager with a lot of family problems, Sara came to SOLVE after she learned that the father of her baby was already married with his own kids. "He wasn't worth my time," she said later of the man who told her to get an abortion but would not give her any money for it.

> "A young woman in the world, so strong, but naïve
> An older man in front of her, only there to deceive
> How could it happen, she says, Why, this to me?"
>
> FROM A POEM SARA WROTE ABOUT HER EXPERIENCE

Her mother had pressed her to have an abortion and Sara considered it, even going to the facility after she scheduled an appointment. But deep in her heart she knew it was wrong and just could not go through with it, a decision that did not sit well with her parents. She came to SOLVE and a lot of that rebellion melted away as she grew up quickly under Sister's guidance. Sara decided she wanted her child to have a family, a father, a college fund — all the things she could not provide. "I knew it was the right thing (to release for adoption), but it was so hard," she said.

> "It's time to go, it's now time to say good-bye
> To only have five days with him,
> As he's carried out the door....She sighs."

When Sister Gloria took her position as Director, there was a policy that once a girl had her baby, she was required to leave the house. It had been that way since the beginning to allow more girls to stay at SOLVE, whose mission was to prevent abortion. The birth of a baby meant that mission was completed. Additionally, the baby counted as a resident minor under their state license so that the mom and her baby took up two spots that might have gone to another pregnant girl in need.

But that wasn't the only reason for the policy. Helen believed that adoption was the best decision in most of the cases and hoped that more girls would release their babies to a loving couple. Allowing the girls to return to SOLVE with their newborns would cause less of them to choose adoption and influence the other residents to keep their babies, too, she thought. Who can resist a darling new baby? And so she adamantly put her foot down. Not even when a house mother went to a Board meeting and begged them to let the girls stay after delivery did she change her mind and her strong opinion swayed the Board. God has asked her to save babies, and that's what SOLVE was trying to do. What happened after delivery would be the mother's responsibility – or another agency's.

Over the years, however —and at Sister's insistence — the Board realized that in order to help the baby, they had to help the mother, too with her transition to life after SOLVE. Few were choosing adoption anymore. As the years passed and having a baby out of wedlock became common, the stigma lessened. Greater emphasis on parenting skills was initiated and the Board finally voted to allow the residents to remain for a short while following delivery while they completed their education or got a job. That pleased Sister Gloria, who worried about what would happen to the girls after they left.

The "bassinette rule" came to be the measure of time a girl could stay — as long as her baby fit in a bassinette, she could continue to live in the maternity home. This was usually about six weeks and gave the new mothers enough time to finish working with the case manager on their future plans as they adjusted to the reality of life with an infant. Most were eager to move on.

Sister Gloria was ready for the next chapter in her life, too. She departed after five years and the Board hired Selena Lewis, a young woman with a social work degree who had actually lived in the maternity home during the time it was owned by her grandparents, who had been friends of Helen's. Ironically, Selena was the first newborn to be brought to the home. Helen couldn't get over it. "To think that little baby is now the Director of SOLVE at the very location she used to live!" she exclaimed, shaking her head at the coincidence.

Selena did not stay very long, however, deciding that the administrative position was not really what she wanted to do. But God had a plan. Under his guidance, SOLVE had finished two decades of saving lives and touching hearts, helping more than 10,000 girls who called on the phone or came into the offices or found a safe place to live in the maternity home.

The 20th Century was soon ending. Who would be the one to take SOLVE into the 21st Century?

Someone was coming who had been working with Helen and SOLVE since the early days of protests at the abortion facility. Someone with a passion for saving babies and an unwavering trust in God that would finally convince the Board that SOLVE was ready to do even more. She just didn't know it yet.

Chapter Ten

God Sends the Right Person

Throughout all the pregnancies and days of raising her children, Donna helped at SOLVE as often as she could, serving on the House Committee and Board of Directors and continuing as a hotline volunteer. Three siblings had joined little Carmen in a few short years. "I can remember being at her house with our kids running around and she would get a call and have to step aside while she counseled someone," said Marla. She and Wilma joined Donna in the SOLVE mission, sharing that involvement along with the joy of their young, growing families.

They treasured those sweet happy days for nearly a decade, although the precious memories would remain forever. Then, on a day that would require all of their faith in God, Al was diagnosed with a brain tumor.

Their older children were attending Bradenton Christian School, where Al taught, when their father began his fight against the tumor. When it looked as if Al would not recover, the superintendent asked Donna if she would take a job as the high school principal's secretary. "I had been working one day a week at a local church, and it was a big change to go to full time work while raising four young children," she said. As Al's health worsened, Donna faced the unthinkable and asked the high school choir to sing at his funeral. She would hear them rehearsing every day at school the song they had chosen, "Great is the Lord," knowing the day was coming soon when they would sing it for the last time.

Al Hoeksema was only 35 years old when he died in 1986. He left behind four children: the girls were 10 and four, the boys six and eight. Donna held him in her arms as he took his last breath and wondered how she would go on. From the time she was a teenager, she had loved only Al.

Donna really wanted to go back home to Michigan; Al had brought them to Florida, but now he was gone and she couldn't imagine staying without him. "But my children had many friends, loved their school, and didn't want to leave," she said. "They asked me, 'Mom, do we have to lose our friends, too?' I couldn't do that to my kids and so we stayed."

The job turned out to be a perfect fit for the young widow. It enabled her to be on site with her children and be home with them when school was not in session, providing for the family until all four graduated from the high school. It was tight, but the little family persisted and as Chad and Nathan got older, they mowed lawns to help with increasing bills. The struggles bonded the family together with a tightness that could never be undone.

Donna's position in the principal's office also gave her years of experience with young people. She met most of their families, too. Students often came to the office and she'd talk to them in her understanding, easy way, encouraging them to stay out of trouble and do their best. They liked her and she liked them, too. She always seemed to know what to say and how to listen, revealing a heart open to teenagers. Having Donna in such a visible position at the Christian school, which drew families from many of the county's churches, also enabled many more to personally hear about SOLVE. Her passion and caring brought them into the mission. Classes collected food while parents wrote checks, provided services for the home and invited representatives from SOLVE to speak at their churches.

It was Wilma who suggested that Donna apply for the position of Director of SOLVE. They had spent many years together on the Board of Directors and now the Board was searching for just the right person to run the program after Sister Gloria's departure. The thought that she might be the one they were looking for simply never occurred to Donna. Surprising as it might seem after all her years of service, she said, "It never entered my mind." However, God's plan was unfolding in a way she hardly expected, although looking back it was so easy to see his fingerprints directing her to this moment.

Donna attended a Youth for Christ event with her youngest child, Allison, who was now a high school senior. Wilma brought her own middle school aged daughter. She recalls what happened when the friends met up: "We were sitting on the floor listening to the speaker talking to the kids about how God has a plan and purpose for your life. He said you have to find your passion. I looked at Donna and asked, 'Why don't you apply for the job at SOLVE?' Donna said, 'I don't have my social work degree,' and I told her she had years of experience working with young people at the school and also on the SOLVE Board and that she had a passion for the unborn. She raised four teenagers and had lots of life experiences." On top of that, Wilma knew that Donna was preparing for the day when she would leave her job. "She always said she would leave when Allison graduated because she wanted another mother to be able to work there."

Timing is everything, they say, and God's timing is perfect. SOLVE founder Helen Cadoret had said many times over the years that God always sent the right person to SOLVE at the right time. "Look at Donna," she would say with a shrug, as if that was all the explanation one needed. After 20 years as a SOLVE volunteer, including three years as Board President, with her children raised and graduated from high school, Donna accepted the position as Director, leading an expansion into the

21st century with passion and purpose that galvanized the entire ministry.

Of course that all happened after the first day at her new job when an overwhelmed Donna put her head down on her desk and asked, "what am I doing here?" She didn't have to wait long to get the answer.

A call came into the office on her second day from a friend in a local mall frantically looking for someone willing to talk with a 17-year-old girl who just discovered she was pregnant. The girl's parents were extremely upset and scheduled an abortion. Immediately, Donna got in her car and drove to meet the girl, all the while pleading with God for the right words to say. Donna listened to the girl as she explained that although she did not really want an abortion, she felt the necessity to obey her parents. "We prayed asking God for power, grace and mercy to take a stand for life. She was receptive to my counsel."

Hearts softened and minds were changed. Six months later, with both sets of grandparents in the room, a healthy baby boy was born. An additional blessing also occurred as the baby's parents got married. Where once there had been a frightened girl facing an abortion, now there was a beautiful little family with hope and a future. If she had had any doubts before, Donna surely knew now that she was right where God wanted her to be.

Chapter Eleven

Living at SOLVE
"A warm, good place to be"

Shivering against her nervousness as much as the blustery wind, the woman who knocked on SOLVE's door was accompanied by her daughter —beautiful, talented, smart, and too young to be pregnant.

The mother said their family situation was already difficult without the added stress of her daughter's unplanned pregnancy. She had been relieved when someone told them about the SOLVE house and gathering courage and what little hope they could summon, they entered the office for their appointment, leaving 17 years of a mother's fondest hopes and wishes for her daughter outside. After filling out the required entrance forms, one of the staff members beckoned them with a smile, "Come, let me show you around."

The mother and daughter didn't know what to expect when they went out of the office and into the maternity home right next door. It certainly looked nice enough on the outside. Walking from room to room, the mother's eyes filled with tears. They were in a difficult situation but the kind people who greeted them and the comfortable, safe home where her daughter would soon live consoled her. Her daughter softly whispered, "Mama, everything is going to be okay."

Every girl needs to know that when she comes to live at SOLVE, although for most it is hard to believe. Compassionate volunteers and staff help her to see that it may be true after all. Their beautiful spirit of welcome — as Helen had insisted from the beginning –along with the cozy house says "we care" in a language every girl can understand.

> *"My name is Maria and I am one of the girls staying here at SOLVE. Since the time of my arrival I have met a lot of nice people. I am pleased to be here because if it wasn't for SOLVE I would probably be in the street. I want to thank everyone that comes to SOLVE as a volunteer and helps out, because you take the time out of your schedule to be here. I see that by doing that, you care and that gives me joy to see people helping others."*

Made possible only by the grace of God, the loving, peaceful atmosphere that one girl described as a "warm, good place to be" noticeably envelopes SOLVE. It can make a life-changing impression on girls like Stephanie, who found herself homeless when her husband was put in jail. Her daughter is now a teenager but it seems like yesterday that Stephanie first walked in the door:

> *"Throughout my stay at SOLVE, I realized that the people I had been associating with were not in the best interest of my child and myself. I had made disastrous decisions about my future up until moving here. I don't think there is any way for me to ever repay your generosity and patience. You gave me the opportunity to change my path."*

Rules and responsibilities help to initiate that change. Every girl has to keep her room tidy, do her own laundry, prepare meals and share general chores such as vacuuming. It keeps the house running smoothly and teaches the girls how to run their own home one day. "You'd have to do these things no matter where you live," said Amber, who thought the rules, including a curfew, were reasonable.

Krista, however, wasn't used to such orderly living. "At first I thought I wouldn't be able to follow the rules, but I have learned to. I would be less disciplined if I were not living here." She said that SOLVE provided an oasis in a chaotic part of her life so that she can now focus on her baby and get the details of day to day living in order.

Ashley found that the structure made things easier. "The restrictions and rules to follow were good; they helped me grow up," said the 18-year-old, who was able to finish high school while living at SOLVE. Having considered her options, Ashley chose to parent her baby and found that it helped to have friends at SOLVE who were in a similar situation. With the other girls she could talk about things common to them. "This baby changed my life," she said. "Having him motivates me to get done what I need to do. He is hard work – but so worth it." She also learned during her stay at SOLVE that God is real. "He is in my life and will help me" – something SOLVE hopes every girl will learn because that is when real change can begin.

All of the girls participate in a weekly Bible study and the church of their choice on Sunday, requirements that model Christian living and help them discover the transforming love of Jesus Christ. The staff has a standard of behavior as old as the Ten Commandments, which a few of the residents were astonished to discover during one evening's lively conversation.

They were having a chat with the housemother, a beautiful young woman who told them she was "saving herself" for marriage. Several of them were shocked. "They couldn't imagine what in the world I did on my night off if I didn't go out and have sex," she later shared with Donna. It gave the housemother an opportunity to talk with them about her faith and God's plan for marriage, revealing why she had made that decision and how she lived her life to serve and please God. Donna calls those opportunities "golden nuggets." "Because we are here 24 hours a day, seven days a week, we have so many moments to mentor and teach, counsel and inspire the girls. We can share our faith in so many ways."

There are other rules to follow, too. Most of the girls who come to SOLVE are not minors; the average age is 19. Those who are under 18, however, are required to attend school and there are a variety of options from which she can choose; a bus even comes right to the door. Like Ashley, some girls graduate from high school – an achievement often abandoned before coming to live at SOLVE – and volunteers are sometimes called on to help with homework or give extra tutoring. "When a smiling girl runs into the office waving a good grade on her test, it's a big step in the right direction for her and makes us all proud," says Donna.

The adult women must have a job or volunteer in some capacity. Helping out at the library or nearby thrift shops benefiting other charities gives them valuable work experience and confidence, not to mention something to put on their resume. Donna's son, Nathan, owner of a Chick-Fil-A restaurant, has thoughtfully hired many of the girls throughout the years. Other supporters have also offered jobs.

Residents can complete their GED or take the course to become a certified nursing assistant or phlebotomist – both programs take less than two months to complete - or begin training for other technical careers. SOLVE even offers scholarships funded by generous donors. A few are able to attend college classes. The opportunities are plentiful for those who take advantage of them. Knowing they can do it is half the battle and often the hardest hurdle to overcome. "Before I came to SOLVE, I thought I was a nobody," said one resident. "Then I met people who made me happy and who made me feel like I was somebody."

Counseling, case management, field trips, parenting

classes, doctor's visits and lots of prayer – all of that and much more goes into each and every day at SOLVE as girls learn how to tackle life's challenges. Sometimes, it's a lesson families have to learn, too.

Parents were investigating SOLVE for their daughter because like so many families, an unexpected teenage pregnancy was more than they could handle. They were amazed to learn of all the programs and help that their daughter could receive at no charge in the beautiful house where she could live for free. They went home and told the grandfather of the family all about SOLVE. "They would do all that for her?" he asked incredulously. "Well, if they can do that for her when they don't even know her, I guess we can do that, too," he said. And they did.

When a girl moves out of SOLVE, she takes everything she has learned into her new life. But each one leaves something behind: the memory of a frightened and unsure girl who arrived without hope and left knowing she is loved by God and that he has a plan for her and her baby.

Chapter Twelve

"Miss Donna, Come Quick!"

Working at her desk, Donna was startled by the urgent tone of the resident who burst into her office. "Miss Donna, come quick!" she said. "Karen's in labor!" Donna was up and running before the word "labor" even escaped from Jenny's lips, racing out of the office and into the maternity home next door. Taking the steps up to Karen's bedroom by twos, heart pumping, Donna heard cries for help coming from the bathroom. She pushed open the door. Terrified, 15-year-old Karen was sitting on the toilet. "I think my baby came out," she cried. "Help me!"

SOLVE had been Donna's life since she prayerfully accepted the position as Director, knowing God had placed her here at this time. She loved her job and she loved these girls, too, who came to SOLVE when they had nowhere else to turn.

Now, one of her girls needed her.

Karen's parents, who lived in another city, placed her in SOLVE so that the schoolgirl's pregnancy would be completed in privacy. She planned to release for adoption. Moaning and frightened, she trusted that Donna would help her, but Donna had never delivered a baby. To complicate the situation, Karen was pregnant with twins, and this delivery was much too early. The babies were not due for another few months. "Jesus, help me," Donna prayed with every cell of her body.

The bathroom of the older home was extremely tiny, and although slim, the six-foot Donna did not have much room to maneuver. She felt her heart pounding and tried to calm herself. She could do this, she told herself, with God's help. "Call 911," she said to Jenny, right behind her. She put her arms around Karen, helping her gently onto the floor. Turning to look into the toilet, Donna was stunned at what she saw. It was a baby.

When the day was done and she finally had a chance to change her bloodied clothes and put her feet up, the sight of that little baby in the toilet filled her mind. The memory would stay with her the rest of her life. Time had seemed to stand still, along with her heart, but God had been in that bathroom as surely as the air she breathed.

Scooping up the baby, a girl, Donna tried to determine if she was alive. So many emotions and thoughts were flooding her mind. Where were the paramedics? Jenny had gotten the 911 operator on the line and she put the phone to Donna's ear while Donna held the lifeless baby. "Rub her chest and put your pinky in her mouth," ordered the operator. Donna did as she was told, praying all the while with an intensity born of fear. Suddenly, the perfect little face scrunched and let out a wail that seemed to come from heaven itself.

"She's alive, Karen, she's alive!"

Overjoyed, Donna shouted in relief as the baby started to suck her finger. Shaking, she reached for a towel and wrapped the newborn, whose mother lay crying and panting on the floor, her work not yet done. Donna had but a second to lay the baby on the bathroom rug before her twin sister came out, catching her just as the paramedics tromped up the steps. They cut the umbilical cords and whisked Karen and the babies off to the hospital. Although small, at a little less than three pounds each, the baby girls were healthy.

The football hero who had taken advantage of the infatuation of a younger girl never learned he had two daughters or the heroic way their lives were saved by a woman who had been working and praying to save babies since before he was born.

Donna had been there at the moment of the precious newborn's first breath. The incredible experience was a counterpoint to what she had experienced so many years earlier, holding her beloved husband while he drew his last breath. It would sear her soul with conviction on the sanctity of human life, which was already an indelible part of "Miss Donna."

Chapter Thirteen

The Girl on the Bicycle

THERE ARE NOT A LOT OF THINGS THAT SCARED DONNA, but putting a girl with an unplanned pregnancy onto a waiting list was definitely one of them. She knew anything could happen in the days or weeks before a bed became available.

As the 1990's came to a close there was continually a waiting list, sometimes with as many as five or six girls on it and even nine at one point. The Board talked about expanding for years but it remained just talk without any concrete actions. They were cautious about finances, knowing anything they received was "God's money," and there was a huge fear that one day they would simply run out of it. "Some were worried that expansion might lead to financial ruin for the ministry," said Jan Schuster, who was one of the newer Board members. "They had been working hard to run SOLVE for more than two decades and didn't want to see that happen."

Helen was 74 and still a very active Board member. Although she recognized the need for more beds, she was not sure how they would pay for another house, even after an extraordinary gift came her way. It happened just a few years before when Gladys Snell elected to donate a portion of her estate to an organization that helped pregnant women. So it was that in late November of 1996 the mail brought a letter from her attorney, along with a check for $113,636. It was the largest gift SOLVE had received in its history and arrived as the Board was considering taking out a loan to pay the few people actually employed by SOLVE, eliciting a collective "whew" from relieved Board members. Treasurer Joan Ruane, who had volunteered alongside Helen from the early years, knew how hard it was to keep the funds coming in. "We were delighted when this bequest came to SOLVE," she said, remembering the financial struggles and constant fundraising of so many years. Mrs. Snell's generosity felt like a reprieve, allowing SOLVE to build up its coffers.

It was less than half of what she would leave them – the final payment of almost $128,000 came two years later, near Christmas of 1998, less than six months before Donna took the helm as SOLVE Director and overwhelming the Board with what to date is still the largest donation in SOLVE history. Although she could recognize God's hand directing them to expand, Helen's fears still gripped her – a new house would double the size of their budget, the original house was old, albeit charming and needed many repairs, the cost of everything would continue to go up, and of course they had to pay for the house. And what about donations? Would they double as well? Helen thought not. They would go through Mrs. Snell's money quickly, and what then?

But Donna was confident in her heart that it was only a matter of time before they opened a second home and soon after the Board hired her as the Director, she began planning for that day. The time drew closer thanks in part to a presidential scandal, a men's pizza and beer night, and a tremendous heartache that shook Donna to her soul. Years later, it is still difficult to tell the story.

"A young teenager rode up to SOLVE on her bicycle," she said. "She was a pretty blonde girl — could have been one of my own kids — and she wanted a pregnancy test. It was positive. She said her father would kill her. We talked for a while and then she rode off on her bike. She went home and told her parents she was pregnant and also about SOLVE, and then the father called me. He was very angry. I asked him to at least come into the office, which he did."

Although he initially was set on an abortion for his daughter, after talking with Donna he decided that she could enter SOLVE if it was kept quiet. He didn't want anyone to know about the pregnancy.

"Unfortunately, the house was full," said Donna. "There was not enough room to take her in. I thought space might open up in a week or so and asked if I could call him back after the weekend." The father called every day that week to see if she could get in. "The next Monday morning he called me and said to take her off the list. 'We took care of it,' he said. I told him, 'Sir, you have just killed your grandchild.'" The man slammed down the phone in anger.

That father was a deacon in his church.

Donna remembers his loud and forceful comment that seemed to explain it all: "This young lady is not going to ruin this family's reputation." She felt like it was a message from all the churches. Did they all feel that way, she wondered? Worried more about reputation and what others would think than in saving the life of a baby? It was certainly a low point for her. Why didn't the Board of Directors hurry up and commit to a second home, she wondered. Where was their faith? Couldn't they see that God would continue to provide?

Devastated, she knew that no matter how difficult it might be or what obstacles they would face, SOLVE desperately needed to build a second home. That very week God used the girl on the bicycle and a national scandal to help the Board commit to the project, and he sent along a man who knew more than a little about building.

Donna had been invited to be the guest speaker for the men's group at Our Lady, Star of the Sea Catholic Church, whose supportive pastor, Rev. Edward Pick, had been a SOLVE Board member for 12 years. His church had paid for the "Choose Life" billboard with SOLVE's phone number located on one of Bradenton's busiest streets. As she drove to the church on picturesque Longboat Key, across the street from the Gulf of Mexico, the turmoil in her heart contrasted with the calm and peaceful waters.

As Donna began her presentation, the men listened attentively. "It was beer and pizza night and me talking about SOLVE. This was during the Monica Lewinsky scandal with President Clinton and one of the members had a relative visiting from Pittsburgh. He had grown tired of watching TV and seeing that story replayed over and over again, so he asked if he could go to the men's meeting to have something else to do." Donna tearfully told them about the teenager on the bike, about her father, about the baby that was aborted because there was simply no more room for another pregnant girl.

The man who was visiting happened to be Dr. Elio D'Appolonia, one of the world's foremost geotechnical engineers and an expert in solving difficult construction problems. He was very moved by Donna's presentation. Touched by the Holy Spirit, he went up to her after the meeting and quietly said, 'When I go home, I am going to mail you a check for $25,000.' "And he did," said Donna, marveling at God's provision. "He did."

The expert in difficult construction problems gave SOLVE more than money – he gave them a needed reminder that no problem, not even constructing another maternity home, was too difficult for God. Helen and her fellow Board members saw that he would continue to bring people into the mission to provide what was needed, and so at last they finally voted to move forward: SOLVE House #2 was about to become more than just Donna's dream.

Chapter Fourteen

"We Wanted a House—God Gave us a Mansion"

Dr. D'Appolonia's generous gift arrived like a memo straight from above, made even more fortuitous since firefighters had just burned down the houses next to SOLVE, leaving plenty of room to build another maternity home.

The SOLVE House was well maintained and landscaped but the house next door had become a blight on the neighborhood. It's boarded up windows attracted vandals, drug dealers and prostitutes who often made the girls and staff feel uneasy. Alice Lauber arrived for her first day of volunteering in the office to find several police cars in the parking lot. Amazingly, the grandmother did not drive away, but bravely got out of her car. "I pulled into the driveway, never having been there before, and the place was swarming with police," she remembers. "This had become a bad area then, with drug deals happening all the time." Alice wasn't going to let that stop her, though, and continued to volunteer along with the rest of the dedicated crew, not to be deterred in their quest to save babies.

When the dilapidated crack house was finally reduced to ashes as the 20th century closed — along with another house on the property which had also been condemned — the entire neighborhood cheered along with SOLVE. Helen ecstatically jumped up and down on the picnic table in SOLVE's backyard shouting for joy. The Board of Directors needed little imagination to see it as the perfect location for another maternity home and they voted to buy the lots.

It seemed a providential omen that Russ Dozeman represented SOLVE at an auction of the property at the County Courthouse on Good Friday, the day Christians recall the death of the Savior, Jesus Christ on the cross. Yet he was outbid by a local attorney representing a group of investors. Although the investors' plan wasn't known, it looked like another maternity home next door was not to be, a puzzling development after all the signs to proceed.

Donna believed the enemy was at work and did not want another house built to save babies. Knowing that SOLVE was God's ministry, as it had been since that day so many years before when Helen heard him asking her to save his babies, she called a friend who had been a missionary and was a strong prayer warrior and asked her what to do. She asked Donna a simple question: "Did you pray over the property?" Donna told her that actually, no she hadn't; she just wanted that property and knew God meant for SOLVE to have it. Well, now was the time to pray!

Donna asked Barbara Gilbert, a woman tiny in stature but strong of faith who would minister to the staff and residents for many years to pray with her. Barbara came right over with holy oil. She and Donna put on their boots and went to the property, still covered with ashes. They walked around the lot repeatedly, praising God and praying fervently for his will to be done with it and that he would forgive all the sins that had been committed there. Standing firm in her convictions, Donna trusted that God would bring it to pass. She knew they might look silly to people passing by, but she didn't care – she just wanted that property with all of her heart. The ladies put a stake in the middle of the lot, claiming it for Jesus, and anointed the stake with oil.

"We Wanted a House—God Gave Us a Mansion"

That night the attorney called to say the property was for sale. Did SOLVE want it?

On August 24, 2001, Treasurer Joan Ruane wrote a check for $45,000 for the property, along with $18,000 in back taxes. All the delays had seemed exceedingly long, yet beyond a shadow of a doubt, God was orchestrating everything in his perfect timing —something they would have to keep in mind throughout the lengthy building process to come.

A big wooden sign, "Future Site of S.O.L.V.E. Maternity Home #2," triumphantly went up on the empty lot and the Board chose June 1, 2002 for the ground-breaking ceremony. It was an historic moment as Helen Cadoret, assisted by Roland, dug into the ground where drug dealers had destroyed lives, breaking ground for the promise of saving lives. Donna, Board president Rita Stormes and 150 guests looked on and cheered, ignoring the blistering June sun, buoyed by the bright yellow mums cascading down the steps of House 1 which the Junior League had so thoughtfully provided. A former resident even came back to cook all the food for the guests. Rev. Vincent Clemente, a Board member, offered the closing prayer and all were confident the home would soon be built.

The many years that Donna had worked at Bradenton Christian School's office now bore abundant fruit. Relationships she had made with so many families and business owners whose children attended the school enabled her to ask for and get many things for free or at cost. Like Helen before her, Donna definitely knew how to ask. Russ Dozeman and his committee had met with Bruce Williams Builders, a prominent Bradenton homebuilder who generously agreed to build the 4,000 square foot home at no profit. They also allowed SOLVE to use subcontractors to do specific tasks. Joe King, a respected local architect who had known "Miss Donna" since he was a teenager, designed the house at no charge. They sat down and Donna just told him what she wanted and what she didn't want and Joe did the rest,

73

designing a stunning home that would anchor the corner of the neighborhood.

The groundbreaking had been held, money was being raised and yet the lot remained quietly empty. They waited for approval regarding water retention and runoff, for repositioning of the house on the lot to allow for additional parking, and for review of the landscape plan with the city, all necessary before building permits could even be obtained. Gazing at the vacant lot next door every day, Donna wondered as the months passed when building would begin. She had waited so long for the Board to agree to a second home and now, more waiting, waiting, waiting — it was a turtle's pace when she desperately longed to be the hare! It was reminiscent of the long wait Helen experienced in opening the first home 25 years before, and Donna kept reminding herself that it was the turtle who eventually won the race. Meanwhile, SOLVE continued to raise funds, determined not to go into debt for the home. Within a year they had raised almost a quarter of a million dollars and it would be completely paid for by the time it opened.

Eleven months after the groundbreaking, the site work began in preparation for building on May 12, 2003. "I never thought a bulldozer would be such an awesome sight!" exclaimed a jubilant Donna, who fairly jumped up and down. When subcontractors came to the property to work on the house, she was right there, telling them all about SOLVE and how this home would be built to help pregnant women. "Where are the men?" many of the workers wanted to know. "Where are the fathers of the babies?" Donna explained that the men just did not want these babies and the women, rather than have an abortion, had come to SOLVE. "That's terrible," they would say, and one by one the subcontractors agreed to do the work at cost. The chain link fence surrounding the property during construction was even donated.

"We Wanted a House—God Gave Us a Mansion"

Eagerly, the staff and residents watched as the house took shape. When summer's drenching rains came, it nevertheless continued to rise. By Christmas the house was in the "home stretch," thankfully; there were five pregnant girls on the waiting list.

On a beautiful spring day, SOLVE's second house was finally finished down to every beautiful detail. Except one. It was Friday, March 12, 2004 and Open House was scheduled for Sunday, but there was no certificate of occupancy....yet. How could that be when a team of six men was already on the road with two moving vans, picking up furniture for the house?

As the staff assembled for their usual morning prayer, aware that there was no CO and praying feverishly, one of the staff members told Donna that she had had a vivid dream about her the previous night. In Reina's dream, Donna was dressed in a suit and headed for work when she got into a terrible car accident. Donna was fine but the car was totaled. She got out of the car, made a call on her cell phone and started walking.

That was all the Executive Director needed to hear. This woman of great faith knew God was in charge. "In my heart I knew he would allow this home to open, so I told everyone to go forward as scheduled. Lo and behold, in walked one of the Board members with the temporary certificate of occupancy, which Bruce Williams Homes had been working all week to secure." As the staff cried tears of joy, they continued unpacking. "'Truly, God turned our mourning into dancing,'" said Donna.

Sunday afternoon before the guests were set to arrive, several dozen Board members, volunteers, family and friends held hands, forming a huge prayer circle from the picture perfect kitchen through the living and dining room and hallway, encircling the gorgeous new home with the faith and love that had made it rise from the ashes. The joy in their hearts fell down their cheeks as one by one they began to pray, choking back tears which few could hide as the power of the Holy Spirit filled the room. Their Heavenly Father had built them a home, putting it all together in an amazing test of faith and bringing it to completion in such a miraculous and beautiful way that all were awed at his power and provision.

"Together we dedicate this new home to God," said Donna. "This is his ministry and all the glory and praise goes to him. The past several years have proven to be a walk of trust and faith in God. Being dependent on Christ gives a believer the amazing ability to maintain a steady ship on a stormy sea. Trust me, there have been numerous stormy moments throughout this building project," she said. "Looking at what God has done, I am amazed. We asked him for another home and he gave us a mansion."

That seemed to be the consensus when the doors were opened and the community came in for a look. After a ribbon cutting with the mayor and other city officials, several hundred guests streamed inside, delighted at the beautiful design and décor. Women from the Junior League had furnished and decorated the seven bedrooms as their major project of the year. As guests strolled through each one, trying to determine their favorite – the rooms were decorated in different themes, from Americana to tropical – a woman was overheard to remark that she thought the loveliness of the home would give the girls a real lift. "It will show them that somebody cares."

The spacious kitchen and gorgeous cabinets earned rave reviews. Originally, the plan was to put standard cabinets in, but because Donna and her husband dutifully drove 30 minutes to pick up a used washing machine that was being donated to SOLVE (even though there was no current need for a washing machine and no place to store it), the donor, who happened to own a cabinet company, heard all about the new house being built and then came to see for himself. He insisted on paying for upgraded cherry cabinets.

Money for the furniture in the living room had been donated, but it wasn't quite enough. Nevertheless, Donna had visited a furniture showroom, picking out exactly what she wanted. "How much is this?" she asked the manager. When he told her the price for the roomful of furniture, she answered that she did not have that much money. They kept dickering back and forth until finally the man said, "Lady, just how much money do you have?" When Donna told him, he replied that she could have all of the furniture she had picked out for that price.

SOLVE House 2 was truly an example of the community coming together to create something beautiful under God's guidance. So many different people, churches and organizations helped in every way — inside and out — from actually building parts of the home to donating furniture, landscaping, and even artwork.

A woman of 90 slowly stepped inside, holding onto her daughter's arm. Many years before her husband had given her four large floral watercolor paintings. They were her most prized possessions. Now living in a nursing home, she had nowhere to put them and had generously donated them to SOLVE. When she saw her beautiful pictures hanging on the wall in the living room, she just stood there and wept for joy.

It was one of the most blessed days in SOLVE's history.

Chapter Fifteen

A Father's Story

SOLVE IS THE STORY OF MOTHERS AND BABIES —but all of those babies have a daddy, too, and sometimes his story is just as remarkable. SOLVE totally changed the life of one of those fathers, a young man named Ben. Or rather, God did. But he used SOLVE – and a baby – to help Ben return to faith and become the responsible father and husband that he is today.

A decade ago, his first child was born to a young woman then living in the maternity home. Life was very different for the businessman and community leader in those days. "I thought I was happy. I thought I was content and that I had it all," he said, remembering back to when his life took a turn he never anticipated. "I had lots of friends and fun, a good job and enough money to keep me happy." A singer and guitarist, Ben played in a punk-rock band that enjoyed some local acclaim. "We were just getting ready to pack up and move to Orlando because we were convinced that we were going to be the next big music sensation."

Ben no longer attended the church of his youth because as he put it, "I saw no need for God at all. I was doing just fine on my own."

One summer evening his on-again, off-again girlfriend, whom he hadn't seen in months, showed up on his doorstep claiming to be pregnant with his child. Ben was stunned. He wasn't ready to be a father and especially not now, with his "big break" just around the corner. The meeting did not go well and Ben suggested she have an abortion. "Why don't we just terminate the pregnancy and go our separate ways," he told her. She didn't agree, and left alone.

In the weeks that followed, he could hardly sleep, tossing and turning as he thought about the baby, his girlfriend, his life. "I couldn't look at myself in the mirror. I wondered where she was." Ben knew that her family situation was rocky and he wasn't sure where she now lived. He remembered hearing about SOLVE during his earlier years in church and considered calling his former girlfriend to tell her about the home — maybe she would consider going there if she was determined to have the baby. He was surprised and relieved when she called him to say she was already living there.

Gradually, it dawned on Ben that ready or not, he was really going to become a father. He had done a lot of thinking. "I started talking with her and discussing just what we were going to do. We talked about adoption, but it didn't feel right. God had begun working in our hearts and we knew we had to keep and raise this child. But we were terrified as to just how we were going to do that. We were just two kids ourselves."

He made it to the hospital just after the delivery of a healthy baby girl. "I will never forget it. I saw her and it was as if the things that weren't so important had the volume turned way down and what really mattered was that tiny miracle in front of me, so helpless." Like millions of fathers before him, Ben was overwhelmed with powerful feelings and emotions he never knew existed. "My heart felt like it swelled to hold the love that I suddenly felt for my daughter. I knew it was my duty to care for and nurture and raise her." Before she even had a name, his daughter had him wrapped around her tiny finger, and that was fine with Ben.

That night the new father wandered out of the hospital into

the parking lot. It was there, under the stars, that he realized he did need God in his life. "I desperately needed his guidance and strength. I sat down on a curb and whispered a long prayer asking God to forgive my arrogance and foolishness and asked for him to show me how to be a good father and equip me to raise my daughter the right way."

There were many challenges ahead: the young couple got married, cared for their baby and eventually were able to buy a small home. "We joined a wonderful church and surrounded ourselves with friends and family who constantly guided, comforted and nurtured us. I will never forget that first year." Two years later, his little girl became a big sister as the family happily welcomed a son.

But something wasn't quite right, although it all seemed just about perfect to Ben. Unfortunately, things shortly unraveled for his wife, who a year or so later walked away from her husband and children for reasons no one really understands. She had simply packed her bags and left. Ben was distraught. She had gotten a part time job and he wondered if something happened at work, if she met someone, if she had become involved with drugs, or if the burdens of their young family were too much for his emotionally fragile wife who had endured such difficult growing up years.

As his children cried for their mother night after night, his heart broke. The now single father clung to his family and his faith: "There is truly no obstacle you cannot overcome with God's help," he said. Over and over he recited Philippians 4:13: "For I can do all things through Christ, who strengthens me," relying on the Biblical promise to carry him through each day. Donna had grown close to the young couple over the years and was just as surprised as Ben when she left without any explanation or reconciliation attempts. He sought her wisdom and strength, dropping into the office to talk and cry and make sense of the heartache that accompanied every waking moment.

Like it always does, somehow life went on.

His daughter, now a budding pianist, is the joy of his life along with his young son, who sleeps peacefully in his Spiderman themed bedroom. Ben remarried a lovely woman. He was invited to join the local civic leadership training program, established to help promising young business people become community leaders. Now in his early 30's, he serves on the board of directors of several local organizations and shares his musical gifts with his church, a bit toned down from his punk rock days. Life is good for the family for which Ben is very thankful.

He is grateful, too for his first wife's stubborn refusal to heed the advice of an immature and self-centered young man – a man who doesn't exist anymore. Instead, there is a man who is sometimes haunted by sobering moments. "I catch myself gazing across the table at my daughter as she sings to herself and colors beautiful pictures of flowers and I think, what if she had been aborted, like I had suggested? What would my life be like without her? What would my life be like if I couldn't watch her sing in the choir or run and play with other children?"

He knows there is nothing he can really do to repay SOLVE for the gift of his little girl, but he tries. He volunteers in countless ways and has introduced many of his friends and business associates to the ministry of SOLVE so that they can help, too. "You are all heroes in my eyes," he says simply.

Chapter Sixteen

A Wild Ride

Working for SOLVE involves wonder and worry, disappointments and drama, tears and triumphs – sometimes all in the same day!

It's a mystery who will walk in the door or call on the phone at any minute, or what will happen next. All kinds of people stop in to take a tour after hearing about the ministry while others bring donations of everything from Bibles to baby clothes, and always there are the girls in desperate need of a home — and who knows when there will be a house mother coming into the office with reports of conflicts that inevitably arise when so many girls from differing backgrounds live together. And of course, almost once a week someone is in labor!

It is unpredictable and even wild sometimes. The staff has grown accustomed to that and knows how to keep everything running smoothly, but once in a while a day comes along when they just hope to survive.

The phone rang and Donna thought the woman sounded desperate. Her boyfriend had just thrown her out, she was pregnant and had no one to talk to and didn't know what to do. It was a familiar story, not much different from the calls that came every day from hurting women looking for help. She asked if someone would be willing to come to her since she had no available transportation.

Donna and Reina Avalos, her assistant, grabbed a map, closed the office and set out to the woman's address in a remote part of the county. They found the dirt road she had described on the north end of town. In the distance they saw an old trailer where they thought she must be living, but to get to her, they needed to open a huge fence which was chained shut. Upon closer examination, they discovered there was no lock to the chain, so together they opened the gate, drove the car in, and then put the chain back in place. They were walking back to the car when suddenly, from the corner of her eye, Donna noticed something moving. Several large barking dogs were quickly charging their way!

Running as fast as they could, Donna and Reina reached the car and slammed the door shut just as the dogs arrived, repeatedly jumping at the car, barking ferociously and terrifying the occupants. Donna could just see the headlines: "SOLVE director mauled to death while making home visit." She and Reina sat for a minute, and then bravely decided to proceed slowly down the long driveway towards the trailer. When they reached the end of the driveway, a woman came out, took the dogs inside and motioned for them to get out of the car.

Praying all the while, Donna and Reina slowly opened the car doors and joined the woman, who was now seated at a picnic table, waiting to tell her story. This was not her first pregnancy; her two older children lived up north with relatives. When Donna asked if their father was in the picture, the woman responded no, he's in jail because of the shooting. Shooting? What shooting? The woman told them he had taken a gun to her head, pulled the trigger and a bullet went right through her skull, coming out the back. Sure enough, she moved her bangs to show Donna and Reina the indentation, which resembled the end of a gun, and moving her hair in the back, there was another scar. Yikes!

Getting back to the pregnancy, Donna asked about her current living situation. According to the woman, her boyfriend's wife kicked her out of the house. Should they be surprised? But, she said, that wasn't the worst of it. That weekend the bar she worked at burnt to the ground so now she was without work on top of everything else. Donna and Reina told her about the SOLVE program and offered her the chance to live there. The woman said she would consider coming to live at the SOLVE house, but that would mean moving to Bradenton.

After patiently listening and offering some other suggestions, Donna and Reina prayed with her and then left. Before returning to the office, they drove past the location where the bar had burnt to the ground because at that point, they were not sure if all or any of her stories were true. On the corner was the remnant of a burnt down bar. They did not hear from her again.

They could not believe how quiet and peaceful the SOLVE office seemed when they returned.

Chapter Seventeen

Peggy

ONE OF THE SOLVE HOUSES NEEDED A NEW HOUSE mother – someone just right, with authority and love, who could keep the house running ship shape. Someone like, well, Mary Poppins, thought Assistant Director Peggy Kerwin. She put out a prayer and an advertisement for just that, pleading "Send us a Mary Poppins, Lord," and waited for God to provide.

It was a rainy day when an applicant whisked into the office shortly thereafter. Closing her umbrella, she opened her mouth to speak and out came the most delightful British accent. Peggy was astounded! She trusted that God would answer her prayer, but this was more than amazing. God had indeed sent SOLVE a Mary Poppins and Peggy half expected her to fly off into the sky when she left after her interview.

Like Helen and Donna, Peggy came to SOLVE because she couldn't ignore God's calling. She and her husband Brian were college sweethearts who lived in California until 2006 when they felt a tug to come to Florida. They weren't exactly sure what they would do when they got there, but in their hearts, they knew that God was leading them to Bradenton. They continued praying about it until the feeling was confirmed by a chance encounter with a stranger at an airport during a layover, with whom they shared lunch. They hardly remember what they ate that day, but they never forgot the incredible conversation in which he talked with them about following

God's plan for your life. And so, they took a leap of faith across the country.

They found a house and enrolled their son, Daniel, at St. Joseph's Catholic School, where Helen's daughters had attended so long ago (the Kerwins' two older daughters were already grown and moved out of the home). Peggy quickly took a good job at a local bank where she earned an excellent salary. One peaceful Sunday afternoon she was relaxing at home and reading the church bulletin when something made her sit up straight: an ad for an assistant director for a Christian maternity home. At that moment, she knew without a doubt why their family had been uprooted. On Monday morning, she eagerly called Donna to interview for the position.

Peggy proved Helen's adage once again that "God always sends the right person when we need it." And SOLVE was definitely in need again. Reina, Donna's former assistant, had said goodbye several years earlier after serving SOLVE wholeheartedly for six years with a beautiful spirit and courage that even ferocious dogs could not deter. Donna could never thank God enough for sending such a faithful helper. Now that SOLVE was growing and modernizing quickly - no longer a simple "mom and pop" type operation – Donna required a strong Assistant Director so that she would feel comfortable leaving the office for speaking engagements and meetings, confident the two homes were in good hands and running smoothly without her.

Infused with a love for God and saving babies equal to Donna's, Peggy was just what SOLVE required. She worked well with her new boss and the two women found they agreed about a lot of things in the business of running SOLVE. They seemed to be on the same wavelength and Donna grew fond of describing her as "the Catholic Donna."

Peggy had moved to Bradenton without knowing a soul, yet she found that God created a family for her at SOLVE. There was Alice Lauber, the spirit-filled grandmother from her church who came into the office every Tuesday to log donations into the computer. With her warmth and affection – and hugs readily dispensed — Alice helped fill the ache in Peggy's heart at losing her own mother years before. He sent others within the SOLVE family whom Peggy came to love as an aunt, a sister, a grandmother. God had called her to leave her home, but he had generously given her a support system, just like he had done for Donna so long ago when Marla and Wilma knocked on her door.

Taking an enormous pay cut to work for SOLVE was difficult for the Kerwin family, yet God continued to meet their needs. Their life seemed so much simpler. Brian was able to spend more time with their teen age son in a way he might not have been able to if they had remained in California, which gladdened Peggy's heart. Watching the relationship of the two men she loved most in this world deepen and develop over Daniel's high school years was a great joy and comfort to her.

Peggy loved helping the girls, although her biggest challenge became knowing when to let go and let God do the rest. Sometimes, Peggy learned, she couldn't help every girl and simply planting a seed was a big accomplishment. It didn't help a girl to make excuses for her behavior or give her time and time again to mend her ways if she was disruptive to the household. Sometimes, Peggy found out, tough love was what it took.

One day, she was showing guests around the house when a resident purposely bumped into one of them, startling the older lady. Quietly, Peggy went up to the girl and said, "Please see me on the front porch. I don't want to say anything in here to embarrass you." On the porch, though, Peggy let her have it, and shortly thereafter, the girl was asked to leave. Surprisingly, every few weeks she came back to talk with Peggy. "You were right," she told her. "I had to learn that for myself and in leaving, I can now appreciate what I had, and know what I did wrong." Peggy kept watering the seed, a little bit every few weeks, watching it blossom.

As Peggy settled in, it appeared that God was orchestrating the SOLVE staff, motivating and drawing them in by his divine appointment. He had sent many willing workers over the years and faithful volunteers who worked in the office, gave pregnancy tests, held babies, ran fundraisers and did whatever it took to keep the ministry going, including putting together the quarterly newsletter after Roland retired from that task. Sherree Parker, a talented layout and design professional, prayed that God would show her how she could use her gifts and new computer to help others. It wasn't two weeks later that a SOLVE Board member approached her. Would she possibly be interested in a volunteer position? Sherree learned that when you ask God, he takes you seriously! "He uses our variety of strengths to carry out his will," said Donna, believing that God has equipped every person with some unique gift. "It's like a tap root and he wants us to go deep with that root to be all that we can be and do for him."

Was his will now calling them to open yet another house? They had been running two homes successfully for four years and still there was not a maternity home in all of Sarasota County, although SOLVE's Sarasota office and "Giving Closet" helped many women every week. Was it enough? Donna had a feeling that God was preparing them to do more and the time was coming when they would learn that she was right.

Chapter Eighteen

"Enlarge the place of your tent"

NOT TOO LONG AFTER THE SECOND MATERNITY HOME opened its doors, one of her prayer partners handed Donna something which she took as a message from God. It was a six-inch tent stake inscribed with Isaiah 54:2:

"Enlarge the place of your tent, stretch your tent curtains wide, do not hold back, lengthen your cords, and strengthen your stakes, for you will spread out to the right and to the left."

Donna didn't need anyone to explain the Bible passage to her — she believed it was confirmation that God was calling her to expand the SOLVE ministry and open yet another home. The Board had learned after the second house was built that God would provide just as he always had, sending more donations and volunteers in ways that would continually remind them who was in charge. This time, it would not take them 25 years to decide to add another one.

The need was urgent — Donna knew that more babies could be saved and more girls helped if there was a home further south. It was a long drive from southern Sarasota County to the downtown Bradenton area where the other two houses were located, which might as well be on the moon for some girls who could not summon the courage to consider a move there, if beds were even available. Many people involved in pro-life ministries in Sarasota County were praying fervently that a SOLVE House would open closer to them.

They compiled a task force of 15 people including representatives from pro-life groups, Pregnancy Solutions (the area crisis pregnancy center, which would eventually refer its clients to SOLVE for housing), several pastors, and Donna and her husband, Curt Vellenga. They met for about a year, discussing the need for housing and how it might be accomplished, reporting back to the SOLVE Board periodically until a Sunday afternoon in 2007 when Donna, Board president Judy Scott and Board member Charles Hall found themselves at a property auction.

Charles, a realtor, had located a piece of property in Englewood –about a 45 minute drive south of the SOLVE Center — including a large home that he thought would fit SOLVE's purposes. By day's end, they had agreed to buy it. In the midst of an economic slump which would worsen over the next year, SOLVE added a third home and for the first time in 20 years had a mortgage – a very large mortgage. All the lessons of building SOLVE 2 seemed to have been forgotten with this newest addition. Soon buyer's remorse spread throughout the Board faster than germs in a preschool. Without enough money in the bank or much of a plan and the quick purchase of a home that may not have been suitable, there would be many anxious moments along the way.

They had purchased a three bedroom house on a large lot with room to expand and plenty of potential. As it turned out, all that potential required a year of work and worry before it could open as a home for four girls, leaving the Board to wonder if they had made a big and expensive mistake. Had they really followed God's direction this time?

A suite for the house mother needed to be built within the house and the screened-in porch enclosed for use as an office. Skip Paschke of Fireside Homes was in charge of the renovations while Jack Seiler, a retired engineer who lived near the house, joined the Board just in time to oversee the project and do much of the hands on work, another example of "God sending just the right person." Linda Porrino had moved from the east coast of Florida to become the house mother because she felt God's call to service. Instead of managing pregnant girls, she found herself directing the comings and goings of workers and volunteers, living in the home through all of the remodeling with a cheerful spirit of optimism.

While church groups and businesses sent volunteers to help with renovations and Curt did everything from hanging curtain rods to chopping down wayward trees that grew too close to the house, concerns about proper zoning and bringing the house up to code kept Board members nervously biting their nails. Would the house even open at all, they wondered. Donna hid her worries and encouraged them to press on, knowing God's faithfulness had gotten them this far — they just had to be patient.

When she wasn't overseeing workers, Linda visited churches in the area, drumming up support. She found a lot of interest in the home; people wanted to help because they believed in SOLVE's mission, and Linda was a charismatic ambassador. Although this new house fell under the general SOLVE budget, it was crucial to find supporters in the area so the budget would not be drained, a real concern for the Board, especially the treasurer, John Yaglenski.

John and his wife, Kathy, were parishioners at Our Lady of Lourdes Catholic Church in nearby Venice which had a very active Respect Life group and a pastor who even joined the SOLVE Board. After retiring from his job as comptroller for a company in Philadelphia, John and Kathy had plenty of time to devote to the pro-life causes they championed, chairing numerous events to help pay the bills. Donna was ecstatic when she visited their church to speak to the women's club and was presented with a check for $25,000 from Elizabeth Deak, an elderly woman who quietly handed her the folded check as the ladies were enjoying desserts and coffee following the meeting. Reaching for her glasses, Donna was stunned when she unfolded the check.

"Glory to God," she thought. "I guess he does want us in South County!" The donation gave them some much needed breathing room.

Breathing nearly ceased, however, when after completely renovating the house to make it suitable for their needs, the county attempted to require them to not only raise the floor of the formerly screened-in porch a few inches to match the rest of the house, but also to install a fire preventative sprinkler system inside the home – both of which would have been prohibitively expensive at that point. Guilt flooded the hearts of some of the Board members who felt they had gotten SOLVE into a real mess with the purchase of this home. Was it just a money pit? Even Donna, a perpetual pillar of faith, was tested.

Fortunately, the officials decided that neither the raised floor nor the sprinkler system was necessary and on September 8, 2008 awarded SOLVE a certificate of occupancy. Pumping her fist and shouting "yes!" a jubilant Donna emailed the Board and task force members to share the good news: "Our fervent prayers have been answered! Today we received notification that Sarasota County has approved us to house up to four residents. To God be the glory! Words cannot express the praise I give to God for allowing us to be his servants in South County... finally!" It wasn't 15 minutes later that a call came in from a girl in nearby Port Charlotte needing a place to stay.

Meanwhile, the two homes back in Bradenton were operating at full capacity and five precious babies had been born the month before, including one lovingly released for adoption. It was a hectic time, yet God's handiwork was evident in the details as they maneuvered through all the trials. "We know this ministry's growth comes during a time of difficult economic conditions," Donna told supporters. "In II Corinthians 9, we are reminded that if only a few seeds are sown, there will be a small crop, but the one who plants generously will get a generous crop."

"ENLARGE THE PLACE OF YOUR TENT"

A very generous gift two months later brightened the Treasurer's mood considerably. Donna had contacted the Templeton Foundation to inquire about applying for a grant and to her surprise Terry Templeton asked to meet her and the staff at the new home. Donna and Stephanie Woodford, newly hired part-time in the office, showed him around and told him about the mission of SOLVE as he listened intently. "Are there any success stories?" he wondered.

Stephanie spoke up and told him that she had been a resident in Bradenton a decade ago, sharing the story of what had brought her to SOLVE and how her life had been turned around – now she had a beautiful nine-year-old daughter, a two year college degree, and a new job she loved. Mr. Templeton was very moved and explained that his uncle, who donated generously to many causes, had decided to focus on grants that not only addressed immediate needs but had eternal value as well. Donna was hopeful when he left after their visit.

Shortly thereafter he announced that the Templeton Board had approved a grant of $38,000 to cover 25% of the annual budget for the house, in part because of SOLVE's track record of success and good stewardship. "We hope even more lives will be changed for Christ because of your ministry," he said. God had used SOLVE to bless Stephanie, and in turn, her story had opened the way for a bounty of blessings for SOLVE.

Managing the newest house from a distance was difficult for Donna, however, just as it had been for Helen when she had to come running over to SOLVE's very first home whenever there was a problem — only this time the distance wasn't five miles; the third house was 42 miles from the SOLVE Center. It wasn't just driving down there for problem solving, however – it was any one of a dozen reasons that took Donna away from Bradenton's two houses and office, including when new supporters wanted to meet her or invited her to attend or speak at a function. She was certainly a wonderful woman whom most people described as "a saint," but Donna had not yet been able to bilocate.

Just like 30 years before, there were some growing pains. But when a healthy six pound boy named Ashton was born two weeks into 2009, all of the troubles were temporarily forgotten — SOLVE 3 had its first baby! Like so many times before, a baby had made them focus on what was most important.

During the next several years they tried a variety of strategies to provide support staff without increasing the budget too much, but it continued to be problematic, as did the costs of keeping the house open. Pregnancy Solutions — the crisis pregnancy center which referred its clients needing housing – soon helped out with a monthly donation of $1800 for a year, providing great relief until SOLVE could get more financially established with business and church partners in the area.

Then along came Kathie.

Hired as house mother when Linda Porrino decided not to stay on after the house opened, Kathie Sullivan Majerchin worked for about a year until she took a leave to care for her terminally ill husband. She came back to SOLVE after he passed away, agreeing to serve as part time Director of Development out of the South County Office, bringing passion, enthusiasm and the expertise she had acquired while working in public relations for a major corporation.

With her great faith and contagious energy, Kathie became the face of SOLVE in the southern county, accepting speaking engagements and developing many new avenues of support. Like Helen and Donna, she too knew how to ask — and she started getting a lot of yeses! She also shared their financial caution and desire to use funds wisely. Worried that the balloon mortgage on the third house would soon burden SOLVE, Kathie set about speeding up the refinancing plans that had been discussed for more than a year. As interest rates plummeted, she visited banks to get the best package in an effort to save hundreds of dollars each month. When a donor contributed $1,500 towards a sign for the house, which the county refused to allow, the money was instead used to pay for the $1,495 appraisal fee — with the donor's approval –as Kathie and the Board merely shook their heads in awe at the gift's timing.

The Board finally began to have confidence that SOLVE 3 was on a firm footing and Donna's burden lifted. It had taken them a while to get there, but things were coming together in God's timing. Which, come to think of it, had always been the way things happened at SOLVE.

Chapter Nineteen

"We Know God Brought Her to Us"

JAHNA KNEW SHE WANTED TO ADOPT A CHILD FROM THE time she was a 16-year-old schoolgirl. The desire in her heart never faded, not even after she and her husband, Larry, celebrated the birth of their son Jerrod. It almost felt like a calling, but when an adoption attempt fell through a few years later, she wondered if it might not happen at all. Little did Jahna know she just had to wait for God's timing and he was already working it out.

For many years the couple served as foster parents to a wide range of kids, giving Jerrod plenty of playmates as he grew up. They also volunteered for SOLVE, becoming role models to the girls, some of whom had little first-hand experience with a happy marriage or positive parenting and needed all the good examples they could get.

When Jerrod was around 12, his mother returned to work full time and the family decided it was time to end their service as foster parents, agreeing to serve as respite care in emergencies. Busy with work and Jerrod's baseball games, they nevertheless agreed to accept a five-month old baby who had been taken away from her mother. "She had the most enormous, expressive eyes. They were striking," said Jahna, fully expecting that the infant would soon return to her mother – a girl who had also briefly been a foster child in their home a few years before.

Juliet Rose, as she had been beautifully named by her mother, didn't go home after that weekend, or the next. For nearly 18 months she lived with Jahna and Larry while her parents attempted to complete the requirements to regain custody of their daughter. Jahna and Larry had contact with both the mother and father — who was nominally involved —but it became increasingly sporadic as time went by, dwindling to almost nothing.

From the first day, Juliet had been a natural fit in the family. Growing through her precious baby stages into busy toddlerhood, developing her friendly and outgoing personality as she learned to walk and talk, she was comfortably at home. When her mother's parental rights were terminated, Jahna knew in her heart that Juliet Rose had it figured out way before they did and God had finally answered her desire to adopt a child.

What Jahna didn't know was that Juliet Rose's mother had been a resident of SOLVE, where she and Larry had volunteered a few years before and whose Board of Directors she had recently joined. The couple wholeheartedly supported the baby-saving mission of SOLVE but little did they know one of the babies saved would become their own daughter. They actually discovered that at a SOLVE Board meeting when Jahna took a seat next to Chris Alexander.

Beaming with joy, she excitedly told Chris about the darling toddler they had recently adopted. "What is her name?" asked Chris. When Jahna replied with her daughter's beautiful and unique name, "Juliet Rose," Chris cried tears of joy. "I have her baby blanket," she replied, and then told the surprised Jahna a story revealing the wonderful work of God in bringing a little girl to just the right family and providing a guardian angel before she was able to go to them.

Chris volunteered in the house at the time Juliet's mother came to stay when she became pregnant a couple of years after aging out of the foster care system. For some reason, Chris was particularly drawn to her. She spent time with the girl and one or two of the other residents, mentoring them and offering a listening ear, sharing her faith in Christ and hoping she was making a difference.

After Juliet's mother left SOLVE with her baby, Chris continued to hear from her. She frequently called Chris for moral support and Chris tried to give her direction. Above all, she prayed. Every day she prayed that the baby would be safe and protected. The mother left Juliet's blanket in Chris' car after one visit and for some reason, Chris did not give it back to her. Now she knew why she had kept it. Chris also had several pictures of the baby and her mother, including one when she was pregnant with Juliet, which she gave to Jahna. "I want Juliet Rose to know that her birth mother did love her, but she just couldn't take care of her. I am so grateful that God answered my prayers for Juliet Rose," she said.

Peggy got to know Juliet Rose quite well the past few years at the baseball games her son played with Juliet's brother. She didn't put two and two together until she happened to take a closer look at the bulletin board in the office filled with pictures of SOLVE babies and children and noticed one who looked very familiar. "I know that little girl," she said, and sure enough, she did. It was the same adorable child who kept all the spectators in the stands entertained.

Juliet Rose is eight years old now and says "I love you, Mommy" so often and with such tenderness it fills Jahna's heart. "We know God brought her to us," her mother says. "All in his timing."

Chapter Twenty

The Story of the Little Breakfast Meeting

"YOU WANT ME TO SPEAK ABOUT SOLVE AT YOUR 6:30 a.m. breakfast meeting? Why, I'd love to," said Donna without hesitation. That's what the director is always supposed to say no matter how much an extra hour in bed is needed and the speaking engagement is an hour away on top of it. Who knew what might come of it? Perhaps a nice check —that happened quite regularly —or an enthusiastic new Board member or volunteer with connections that would benefit SOLVE.

Donna had learned over the years that every invitation came with promise and possibility and so she was determined to make the most of each one, remembering the $25,000 that had been given to her at the church in Venice after addressing their women's club, and the $25,000 check she got in the mail from the Pittsburgh man who had heard her speak so passionately. She never turned down an invitation to represent SOLVE because you just never knew. So, when the invitation from the Sunrise Kiwanis Club came, Donna set her alarm for an extra early wake-up, thinking of the remarks she planned to give.

Normally there would be about 20 people in attendance, they had told her, but when she walked into the restaurant after an hour's drive just as the sun's rays began to color the sky, she greeted an audience of three people. They apologized for the low turnout. It wasn't the first time Donna had experienced that so she just started talking with the passion that had made her such a gifted and popular speaker. The breakfast trio was very interested in hearing about SOLVE, wanting to know all about the girls and the babies, listening intently, asking questions and learning more in such a small, intimate gathering than perhaps they might have if all members had been able to attend.

While driving back to the office, Donna inquired of the God whom she served so faithfully, "Now, just what was that all about?" She didn't mind getting up early, but driving a total of two hours to speak to three people? Still, she had done what she was asked to do, and in her long experience with SOLVE —and the Lord — that mattered.

Several months later Donna was invited to write a grant request to the club and received $700 for a new washer and dryer. It seemed that the little breakfast meeting had been worth it after all. But unbeknownst to the faithful director, that was just the beginning of an incredible story she never could have imagined in her wildest dreams. Like all great stories, it had a cast of diverse characters yet to be introduced which would slowly unfold over the next year and a half, and a plot that would take some surprising turns before the final chapter.

Calvary Chapel of Sarasota invited Donna to speak at their early Sunday morning service about a year later and, just like the breakfast meeting, she found the attendance was extremely small compared to their average worship services. Afterwards, Donna stood by the main entrance shaking hands with everyone. A gentleman took her hand and said, "Do you remember me?" Fortunately, Donna did recognize him and his name came right to her. "You're John Moore from Sunrise Kiwanis Club!" He told Donna the Sunrise chapter was merging with a larger club and they had some funds which needed dispersing. The club members with whom she had shared that early breakfast had immediately thought of SOLVE.

The following Saturday Mr. Moore and the other two members came to Bradenton for a tour of the maternity homes. Impressed, they asked what SOLVE needed. "We could really use a new vehicle for the south county home," Donna answered, explaining that SOLVE needed safe, reliable transportation to get its residents to their medical, educational, and employment commitments. The vehicle for House #3 was always breaking down, a constant worry and expense. Uncertain of their decision, the club members promised to contact Donna after they thought about her request.

On Monday morning Donna turned on her computer and clicked on an email from John Moore. They had decided to give $15,000 to SOLVE for a vehicle! Elated, she finally had the answer to her "what's this all about, God?" inquiry.

Wanting to bless those who blessed SOLVE, Donna contacted the Templeton Foundation, which had awarded SOLVE $38,000 the year before as part of its mission to faith based ministries furthering God's kingdom. Their family ran an auto dealership in Ft. Myers. She and Peggy took off on the 90 mile drive to look over their inventory of vans, hoping they would find something to purchase and thus repay their generosity.

They did find just the right van but it cost $20,000, five thousand over the amount they planned to spend. The ladies thought they would have to keep looking, but the Templetons agreed to sell the one-year-old Toyota Sienna van in "like new" condition with a full warranty out the door for the $15,000 they had been given by the Sunrise Kiwanis Club.

What a story!

The concluding chapters were still being written, however. As it turned out, there had been a lot more happening at Calvary Chapel that recent Sunday morning. An older woman in the congregation had been listening very carefully to the story of SOLVE. A few days later she came to the office to see for herself and investigate the possibility of volunteering in some way. The white-haired woman had her own incredible story to tell.

Sitting down with Donna, she told her that when she was 17 years old and living in Germany, she was raped and became pregnant. She gave birth to a baby boy but he was taken from her and she was sent away to relatives living in America. Without her knowledge or consent, her grandmother signed for the baby to be adopted. He was the only child she would ever have and she deeply regretted that she had not been allowed to raise him. Hearing Donna's talk ignited her compassionate desire to help girls in unplanned pregnancies so their outcome would be happier than hers had been so many decades before.

What happened next was a story of how sometimes events happen in a person's life that are difficult to understand at the time, but which God can use to bring about great things for him. Because of this courageous and compassionate woman who sought to help others, blessings rained down on SOLVE in a way that met a great need and nourished their spirits.

After spending time with some of the residents, she told Donna about a young couple from church she wanted Donna to meet and arranged for them to tour the maternity homes. The man's last name was Yoder, familiar to everyone in town for their delicious Amish cooking and secretly Donna hoped they would bring one of their famous peanut butter pies! Paul and his wife, Mandy, were deeply moved by what they experienced at SOLVE as they saw all that was being done to help girls in need, but they hadn't brought a pie — much to Donna's disappointment. Her mouth had been watering for the gooey and delicious dessert!

Before leaving, Paul wanted to know what SOLVE needed most. Witty house mother Janet, sensing an opportunity, quipped, "Well take my van. The electric windows don't work, the brakes squeak, the air conditioner rarely works — it's a mess!" She was right; in fact, Donna had been pleading with the Lord for a safe and reliable vehicle for House 1 for quite a while.

As it turned out, Paul was not part of the restaurant Yoders, hence, no pie. But he did just happen to own Yoder Auto, which made Donna's thoughts of pie quickly vanish. Something was happening here – she could just feel it.

"Give me the keys," he said, promising to either fix the van or get another one for SOLVE. Four days later on September 8, 2010, he returned, pulling into the parking lot in a beautiful blue Chrysler Town and Country van, just two years old with low mileage. "It's yours," he said, as Peggy ran out with her camera. Two days later he brought back the old van, which he had repaired.

SOLVE received at no cost two beautiful vans in two short months and a refurbished van as an extra, all because of Donna's yes to a couple of early morning speaking engagements the year before. Two weeks later Mr. Yoder completely surprised the SOLVE staff when he drove up in a bright red 2009 Chrysler Town and Country van. He had learned that the other van used by SOLVE was too large and cumbersome for pregnant women to get in and out of easily, especially with babies in car seats, so he gave them another one.

The summer of three almost new vans – one for each maternity home — was an enormous encouragement for everyone at SOLVE.

They could hardly believe it. Watching in awe as God worked in the hearts of their supporters, they were reminded once more who was really writing the SOLVE story. Following a difficult year of expansion, it truly seemed to be a reward, a thank you from the heavenly Father who always knows what his children need.

SOLVE needed vans and encouragement, and got them both in a storybook ending they would never forget.

Chapter Twenty One

"The World You Don't See"

Roland Cadoret described SOLVE as made up of "the world you don't see. It's people living these different lives which, unless you are in an organization like SOLVE, you don't even realize they exist."

"Different" to Roland meant a tragic departure from the American dream of a normal good life such as he and Helen enjoyed – everything he had fought and suffered for in World War II —and he never ceased to be amazed at how many of them existed. Girls like Lisa (not her real name), whose fresh faced complexion and long blonde hair might cause one to mistake her for a high school senior anticipating the prom when she is actually a 24 year-old alcoholic midway through her fifth pregnancy.

Just like most of the girls who come to SOLVE, Lisa hoped for someone to love her, but since she had been given so little love in her life, she didn't know what real love meant. Her story may seem extreme although much of it is similar to what other residents have experienced in "the world you don't see." It is a world which, unfortunately, has expanded with the escalation of drug abuse and fractured families.

When her mother was killed in an auto accident, two-year-old Lisa's father was left to raise his child alone. His relatives mistakenly thought this would help him "grow up," but in reality the problems were only beginning, extending far beyond mere immaturity to alcoholism and drug use. She endured many years of physical and mental abuse due to her father's drunken rages. "He was always angry and bitter," she remembered sadly, telling her story matter-of-factly. Throughout her childhood, Lisa went back and forth between her father and an aunt out of state and even had a stepmother for a short time.

In her middle and high school years she used alcohol and marijuana right along with her father, who readily shared with any of her friends who came over. "They thought it was cool that my dad gave them alcohol and pot. Their parents hated my dad and wouldn't let their kids come to our house, but they came anyway. I knew then I was an alcoholic, but was powerless to stop."

Lisa's first pregnancy happened when she was 17. "I wanted the baby, but the father didn't seem to care. My friend was having an abortion, so I had an abortion, too." She soon fell in love with a 28-year-old man who became her husband and the father of four of her children – the first was already on the way. "He almost immediately started saying we had to give the baby away," she said. Lisa didn't understand why Ron (not his real name) did not want his child, but she did not have the strength to stand up for herself and reluctantly signed adoption papers.

When she became pregnant again Lisa was determined to keep the baby and Ron consented, but the violent pattern of her life continued when the infant was soon discovered to have a broken ankle and fluid on her brain. Although Lisa did not suspect Ron of harming their daughter – he told her the baby had rolled off the sofa —the authorities removed her from their home, placing the baby with Ron's mother.

The devastation of losing another child drove Lisa to using drugs and alcohol again and she and her husband spent a brief stint in jail. Several months later, out of jail and apparently off drugs and with good intentions, the couple got an apartment and both were working. Lisa made peace with the fact that her daughter was living with Ron's mother. But this relatively tranquil stretch did not last.

Several years later, the couple had another baby. "She was screaming one day and he wouldn't let me have her," Lisa says. "I pleaded with him. She was holding her arms out and she wanted to come to me." Then, as if what she's about to say is too painful to recall, too much for her to believe, she says quietly, "He kicked me in the stomach and I went flying across the room." She says that later he apologized. Lisa did not leave Ron then. "It has been that way my whole life," she said by way of explanation, knowing it is hard for most people to comprehend.

Shortly thereafter, Lisa noticed that her baby, on medication for a respiratory infection, appeared to have swelling on one side of her face and she rushed her to the hospital. There, under the bright lights, Lisa noticed bruising on her scalp and tests revealed that the baby had three skull fractures and brain bleeding. "I fell on the floor screaming and praying to God to let my baby live," she said. At first the authorities thought that she had harmed the baby and police questioned her, however her husband eventually made a confession and was arrested for aggravated child abuse. Their daughter, now fully recovered, was also placed with Ron's mother.

This time Lisa did leave her husband. "I looked for a man who was opposite my father and found a man who was just like him." For a time, she lived at a shelter for battered women. Pregnant with Ron's baby when she left him, Lisa decided to have an abortion but she missed her appointment, which she felt was a sign from God. She came to SOLVE where she is receiving counseling, going to drug and alcohol classes and will soon join a support group for women who have been battered.

Lisa is carrying a boy this time.

Despite all of her heartache, she hasn't relinquished her dreams. She wants to go to college to become a social worker or a drug counselor. She wants a home and her independence, and most importantly, Lisa wants to be allowed to keep this baby and to get her daughters back. "All my hurt has made me who I am," she said.

It is hard to comprehend everything she has endured in her brief 24 years. Girls like Lisa are so broken that living a normal life as Roland enjoyed is almost impossible, but SOLVE has learned time and time again that all things are possible with God. The love of Christ can heal the hurt that so many carry and perhaps that is why he brought her to SOLVE where she can begin to see the light. Not just see the light, but feel the warmth through the compassion of the people who surround her and care for her, where she can finally begin to understand what real love means.

It is easy to be overwhelmed but Donna and the staff and volunteers have learned to take it day by day, one resident at a time, beginning with prayer, knowing that God is in control. "With each new resident at SOLVE, I repeatedly become aware of the battles waged by others," she said. "Working with these young, pregnant women who have chosen to bring their unborn baby to life, facing incredible odds, makes me humbly grateful to God for the unmerited blessings I have in my life."

Roland was right. "The world you don't see" is not a pretty place and most people would not want to visit it. Helen's philosophy had been (and her pamphlet had stated), "There but for the grace of God go I." SOLVE offers an escape from that invisible world into the world of God's grace, even for girls like Lisa.

Chapter Twenty Two

Glitz, Galas and the Quarterback's Mom

When Fr. Moretti picked up a pen and wrote a check for $500 to initiate Helen's organization, it was just the beginning of a need for funds that would grow through the years. Putting Christ first, SOLVE refuses city, state and federal monies and the restrictions that come with them. SOLVE was also turned down by the local United Way because of its Christian emphasis and requirement that the residents attend church, yet there is always enough to run its three homes and pay the dedicated staff their modest wages.

Sometimes it seems miraculous. How else to explain the gentleman who walked in one day with a check for $10,000? He was only in town for a business meeting and while reading the morning newspaper he came upon an article about SOLVE. Being a man who happened to have a foundation that sought to address the needs of women and children, he found the article extremely interesting!

"God has never, ever let us down," says Donna, who is just as frugal – and faith-filled —as Helen had been.

Like most non-profits, SOLVE is forever running a money maker of some kind. For those with eyes of faith, it seems that their heavenly Father sometimes arranges fund raisers to especially delight the staff and volunteers — perhaps as a special thank you for the incredible work they do for him – like the time SOLVE appeared in a New York Times best-selling book.

Thinking "nothing ventured, nothing gained," Chris Alexander, an avid reader of Karen Kingsbury's many popular Christian fiction novels, had written to the author requesting that SOLVE be considered for her "Forever in Fiction" charity donation: The winning bidder would become a character in one of her upcoming books. Chris was thrilled when SOLVE was selected.

It came up for auction at the 2007 Gala fundraising banquet where Gayle Flynn bought it in honor of her husband, Tom, an attorney and past president of the SOLVE Board of Directors. Friends of SOLVE could hardly wait for the book to be written and wondered what character Tom would be — Gayle expected her husband's character would be "the plumber, the chauffeur or something else very trivial." Who could imagine how it would all come together? SOLVE was going to be in a real book by one of the country's most popular authors!

Two years passed and the book was forgotten until *This Side of Heaven* debuted on the New York Times bestseller list early in 2009. The author had written a two page dedication about the Flynns and their auction purchase to benefit SOLVE, noting that "Thomas's character in *This Side of Heaven* is that of a godly personal injury attorney, the one who demonstrates through fiction the importance of having godly men to represent those who are wrongly injured." Tom's character was featured prominently in the book, thrilling the staff and board members who could hardly believe what they were reading.

In mid 2009, well before the media firestorm about the Super Bowl Commercial, SOLVE booked the mother of quarterback Tim Tebow to speak at the March 2010 Gala, "Imagine the Possibilities," its biggest fundraiser of the year. Pam Tebow was certainly familiar to the University of Florida football fans when SOLVE scheduled her to speak, but by the time the event came around, she had become a prominent national pro-life spokeswoman. "Who would have guessed a year ago when Pam Tebow was selected to be our speaker that her name would command such attention with the national press?" marveled Donna. "God has provided a golden opportunity for SOLVE. We may draw people to the Gala because of their interest in Pam, but by the time they leave they will be moved by the mission of how we come alongside young women who bravely made the same choice that Pam did."

When Tim became the first sophomore to win the Heisman Trophy, the fact that his mother had contracted an illness while pregnant with him in the Philippines and that the doctor had advised an abortion became nationwide news, along with her brave decision for life.

In the months leading up to the Gala, she became a household name as the announcement that Focus on the Family was producing an ad for the upcoming Super Bowl starring Pam and Tim stirred controversy. Although no one really knew what was going to be in the ad, it was instantly attacked by abortion supporters who resented the Tebows' stand for life as part of their Christian beliefs. News media around the nation and beyond reported endlessly on the ad and whether it should even be aired. The New York Times even published an editorial supporting the ad, saying that the protest by pro-abortion groups was "puzzling and dismaying." The Tebows had become part of a huge national story.

When the Super Bowl game aired the month before the Gala and the widely anticipated ad was finally shown to the nation, everyone wondered what all the fuss had been about. There was nothing controversial about it at all. Yet the "fuss" had galvanized more people into a defense of human life, opening discussions and bringing an issue which is often relegated to the "Letters to the Editor" column onto the front pages and into the living room.

Because of her busy speaking schedule, Pam arrived at the Tampa Airport just two hours prior to the Gala. Donna and Peggy offered to be her chauffeur, maximizing every minute together, knowing a hurried stop at the two Bradenton maternity homes was essential if Pam was to capture the heart of the SOLVE ministry. It worked. She expressed her sincere amazement not only at the beauty of the homes, but the sweet spirit she sensed inside both. And that evening she delivered a message from a mother's heart, with stories of her family, her faith and her belief in the sanctity of life that, as Donna had foretold, brought many new supporters into the fold.

SOLVE couldn't have afforded the tremendous publicity her appearance generated, a testimony of God's timing, his providence and his love. Who could have imagined the possibilities when it all had been planned?

Chapter Twenty Three

Forever Grateful

> "Just wanted to say hi and let you know I used to live at the SOLVE house in 1986 until my son was born. Having had an abortion before him, the mental anguish was more than I could bear to handle again, so I decided to put him up for adoption, but the first time I felt him kick, I knew I couldn't live without him in my life. We (my mom and I) kept him and I am so glad we did! He is now 20 years young and such a gentleman – a true blessing in our lives. We can't imagine life without him!
>
> Thanks to SOLVE, I am forever grateful!! I keep you all in my prayers.
>
> God Bless,
Sharon
(published in May 2007 newsletter)

LIKE SO MANY YOUNG WOMEN OVER THE DECADES, Sharon's joy at being a mother was all because of SOLVE. Recently she came back to volunteer, bringing other women from her church group to pamper the residents with haircuts and massages. "I was taken back with nothing but good memories as I visited my old room. It made my heart sing to be there helping at the place that helped me!"

"Making hearts sing," as Sharon so eloquently expressed it, is what SOLVE does best, with God's help:

"Sing to the Lord a new song, for he has done marvelous deeds."

—Psalm 98

Grateful girls show appreciation in a variety of ways for all that God has done in their lives through the ministry of SOLVE. Some call or come back to visit months or even years later just to talk, to seek advice, or to show off their beautiful children. A former resident who had moved out of state was vacationing in Orlando with her three-year-old son and made the two hour drive to Bradenton to say thank you. She was in her thirties when she left everything up north to start a new life in Florida, unaware that she was pregnant. Her immediate response was to have an abortion, but every day as she traveled to work, her eyes were drawn to Father Pick's billboard: "Choose Life" it said in big, bold letters, with SOLVE's phone number underneath. Day after day the words spoke to her until one afternoon she dialed the number and came into the office to learn what SOLVE had to offer. "By the end of our conversation, she embraced the fact that no child is a mistake and chose life for her unborn baby," said Donna. And here she was, three years later, driving 100 miles to visit and say thank you to the ones who had made that understanding possible.

A girl who had been distraught to learn she was pregnant turned out to be especially thankful that she had come to SOLVE for a free pregnancy test one Friday afternoon as Donna was cleaning off her desk to go home for the weekend. She cried, telling Donna that she was determined to abort if the test came out positive because she was not ready to be a mother. As she hurried out the door following a positive test, Donna calmly reminded her that she already was a mom. "You don't understand," she screamed in reply. Donna went home disheartened, but knowing that she had done her best. Months later, the same young lady returned, cradling her newborn daughter. "Thank you for telling me I already was a mom," she said. "It made me think and now I don't know what I would do without my baby. She is my life."

A woman approached Donna after a presentation at a church, handing her a check. She said that 23 years ago SOLVE was the only place who offered her diapers and formula for her newborn.

Occasionally, the door opens and a woman steps inside saying, "Do you remember me?" Donna's memory is excellent – a trait she shared with Helen – although sometimes it takes a little prompting. But one day, she just couldn't place the woman who came in with a donation, asking to see the inside of House 1. As they walked from room to room, her eyes glistened with tears. Twenty years previously she had been a resident and she was now coming back to begin a healing process. "If it wasn't for SOLVE, my son would not be alive," she said.

Many girls kept in touch with Helen throughout the years, writing letters and calling her on the phone – some even visited to reminisce with the woman they considered family. "You're my mother," one former resident lovingly wrote on the card that accompanied a "World's Greatest Grandma" balloon bouquet. "I'll never forget you." Helen's daughter Carollyn remembers many knocks at the door of the little cul-de-sac house. "They would tell my mother, 'You may not remember me,' and pull out pictures of their children to show her," she said. "You wouldn't believe all the people who have pulled up in that driveway over the years." Every mother knew it was due to Helen's faithfulness to God that her child had been born.

In the fall of 1998, a letter stuffed with photos arrived from a woman who had lived at SOLVE 15 years earlier. Happily married with two children, she wrote:

Hi Helen and Roland,
  We are enjoying our lives now and there is so, so much to do! Thanks be to God! Melissa is in 9th grade, doing well and is continuing in her ballet lessons. She's been on "point" now for a

few years. A scholarship she received for it back in '96. Tonight I have to go to a P.T.A. meeting. The fall is here now and it's the "peak." I love it!

Take care and I'll write again soon.

Love,
Diane
XXOO — SOLVE '83
P.S. "The value of life is a family."

The XX'es and OO's tell the story of a woman who never forgot those who helped her when she needed it the most.

SOLVE occasionally receives letters of thanks like the one sent by the mother of a resident:

"To the SOLVE Staff: Just a little note to let you know how grateful we are for your kindness, understanding and love towards our daughter. Words cannot express my gratitude. I have come to think of you as family. Thanks for sticking by us through our most difficult time.

Letters arrive, too when a baby starts kindergarten, makes a First Communion or celebrates another happy milestone. In July of 1994, the newsletter published a photo of a boy identified only as "Steve Handsome." His grateful mother had been SOLVE's very first client when they opened in that Bicentennial summer and along with the picture she enclosed a note: "He just graduated from high school with honors and plans to enter college this fall."

Kerri's story is one of SOLVE's more memorable in recent years, and not surprisingly, gratitude fills her heart. "I am so grateful to the women at SOLVE," she said. "They saw the light inside of me that I didn't know was there." Before coming to SOLVE, Kerri had been to college twice but could never find her "path to success" as she phrased it. She was 24 and living with her boyfriend who already had two children from his previous relationship. Because he had no car and no job, Kerry worked to support the two of them, but her meager earnings often left them with little money for food. "I had a very negative spirit; I had negative habits, negative relationships and a negative view of myself. At the very lowest point in my life, when I wasn't sure if I could even survive myself, I got pregnant. I had no job, no support and nowhere safe to live. My mother lived in a 55-and-older community and could not take me in. She mentioned a group home called SOLVE and told me she would check it out with me. This would be my first lesson, to become humble."

Kerrie learned not only that lesson, but many others as well, quickly adapting to the SOLVE program. Like someone thrown a life preserver, she recognized the opportunity she had been given and made the most of it, taking every pre-natal, parenting, nutrition, Bible study and faith development class or seminar SOLVE offered. "I went from not knowing if I could make it another day to being excited about my life. I have given my life to the Lord. I even felt my baby move for the first time during praise at my church!"

The staff joyfully watched Kerri's transformation. "Seeing this confident young woman emerge from her broken shell is a testament to what God can do in a life, if only given the opportunity," said Peggy. Kerri earned a phlebotomist license at SOLVE and received a college scholarship. She has since completed an associate's degree in liberal arts and is working towards a bachelor's degree in health services administration while employed as a medical office manager. "Going to SOLVE was the best thing that ever happened to me."

Not too many SOLVE girls miscarry but unfortunately Tiffani did and left the program. However, she continued her education and emailed these words of thanks, revealing all she had learned during her brief time living in the maternity home: "Since SOLVE, I've been keeping God as a big part in my life. I passed my GED test and now am looking into colleges. I'm thinking about getting a degree in counseling and maybe work in the correction system to help kids turn their lives around like I did. It would be such a rewarding job to help someone, like you guys helped me. You made me feel like I can go somewhere with my life when I never thought I could, and you were there for me when I had no one. My due date was supposed to be in a few days. It's been getting to me, but I know that no matter how much it hurts, God has a plan."

Expressing wisdom unearned by many twice her age, this young girl said it exactly right — God does have a plan. Even when his children deviate from that plan, he is always creating a new plan filled with marvelous deeds if they only trust in him, a lesson the staff is always trying to teach. That Tiffani was able to learn this during her time at SOLVE was more than enough thanks for them.

Chapter Twenty Four

Saying Goodbye

"GOD BE WITH YOU" PEOPLE USED TO SAY TO EACH OTHer when leaving, expressing a prayer that the Almighty would safeguard them as they departed. Over the centuries it became shortened so that our familiar goodbye is all that remains. Few remember its original meaning, but that prayer of farewell expresses what the staff hopes for each girl as she walks out the door for the last time and into her new life. They have invested so much of their heart into her — now it is time to let go and let God.

For the girls, saying goodbye to the compassionate staff and volunteers who care so much is never easy. "The hardest part about our program for most of the residents is leaving it," says Donna. "Of course it's hard for us, too. We become very fond of some of them."

Every resident works with a staff member during her stay whose job it is to help her plan for life after SOLVE. Maria Houston, Client Services Coordinator, guides each girl as she investigates all the possibilities and reaches a decision. Her baby's birth puts that plan into action, although it can be anywhere from several days to several months before she moves out. Those who choose adoption leave with the chance to make a fresh start, taking hopeful plans for the future as one girl from Chicago experienced. She didn't want anyone to know about her pregnancy, released her baby to a delighted couple, and returned to school in time for her senior year.

Although the stigma of unwed motherhood has greatly lessened since SOLVE first started helping girls in 1976, the financial hardships have not, and so the best option is usually for the mother to move in with someone else, whether relatives or an organized program. Some return to family members who have had time to adjust to the idea. Linda's parents angrily threw her out after she refused to get an abortion, yet many months later when the baby was born — their precious new grandchild — they welcomed both into their home with open arms. Linda wasn't the only one who had changed.

Other girls enter transitional housing programs that help young moms with children. SOLVE works closely with these organizations to insure a good match, including Our Mother's House in Venice which accepts many of SOLVE's residents. It is a two year program supported by the Catholic Diocese where girls can live with their baby while finishing school or working to save money. Danielle moved into Our Mother's House after she graduated with honors from high school, just six weeks after giving birth to a baby girl. Another young woman recently qualified for a Habitat for Humanity house after finishing the program at Our Mother's House.

Justina, 20, never lived at SOLVE but came into the office looking for free diapers for her two-year-old boy. She was also pregnant with a child she planned to release for adoption. "I told Donna that I had dreams of making a better life for myself and my son. From that day on, she was like an angel guiding me towards those dreams. She set up my interview at Our Mother's House and even drove me there. Later, when I was able to move in, Donna and her husband Curt helped me move. I can honestly say that without SOLVE or Donna, I don't know where I would be right now."

There are not enough places of this sort, however, and as this book is being written, exciting things are happening

– God seems to be leading the ministry to expand into a transitional housing program where girls can continue with what they have learned at SOLVE.

Occasionally a girl will get her own apartment, or reunite with the father of her baby and once in a while someone even gets married. Fortunately, for most residents, what they have learned at SOLVE prepares them to live a better life with their baby when they do say goodbye. As Donna firmly believes, "The baby is not the problem. It's all the other 'stuff' in their lives including bad decisions." Sometimes families have a lot of other "stuff" going on, too.

Susan was almost 20 when she came to SOLVE needing shelter because her mother had asked her to leave. A daughter's pregnancy can be the proverbial "straw that broke the camel's back," especially in a fragile family situation, already tottering with too many trials. Something has to give, and often, it's the pregnant daughter. That's what happened to Susan. A typical girl from a nice family, she had the misfortune to become pregnant at a very difficult season of her family's life: her father had just died, her mother was overwhelmed with his loss and her own health issues and on top of that their home was in foreclosure.

SOLVE provided Susan with a happier place to live while she figured out her future and gave her mother space to deal with all of her own problems. In time, mother and daughter both figured it out and they reconciled. SOLVE said goodbye to Susan knowing she was on the right path and she went on to finish her college education, becoming a teacher. One day she brought her mother to visit and as they drove along, Susan excitedly pointed out, "Look, that's one of the churches we went to and that's a store where we used to shop."

Some girls leave SOLVE with the high school diploma or GED they earned while living there. It might not sound like much, but it is a necessary first step not only to further education, but also to employment. Others have earned their certified nursing assistant certificate, enabling them to get a better than average paying job in a field where jobs are plentiful in Florida.

While some girls disappear into their new life, others keep in touch after they say goodbye and sometimes former residents turn up when you least expect them. Donna and another staff member were standing in a store check-out line when a customer excitedly noticed her name badge, exclaiming "I lived at SOLVE!" She said that her husband was in the Army and that her parents, with whom she was temporarily living, pressed her to get an abortion, which she did not want to do. She told Donna that her husband's Catholic parents urged her not to have an abortion. After talking more with her husband and his parents, she found out about SOLVE and came to live there. "My husband died two years later," she stated, "but my daughter is now 21 years old!" Finishing her story, she jotted her name and phone number on a piece of paper and handed it to Donna. "Let me know if there is ever anything I can do for SOLVE."

Not every girl goes on to live happily ever after. A small number are so damaged that their time at SOLVE is just not enough to undo a lifetime of pain, including sexual abuse, parental rejection, endless foster homes, or even violence, no matter how hard the staff tries.

Sometimes SOLVE has simply been the first step for them in the release of God's grace, yet, while they are living in the maternity home they are loved, respected and counseled — it's a beginning.

One of the rare girls who had to be exited from the program because of her foul attitude and language — which nothing seemed to improve — later mailed a Mothers Day card to the surprised housemother who had done so much for her. A seed had been planted — perhaps someone else will come along in her life to help it blossom. That's part of the letting go and letting God that is so difficult but necessary for the staff, yet they do it, acknowledging that God is in control and they have done their part.

No wonder it is so hard to say goodbye. God be with you, SOLVE girls.

Chapter Twenty Five

Still, By His Grace

"For I know the plans I have for you, plans to give you hope and a future, declares the Lord."

Jeremiah 29:11

SOLVE's mission since 1976 has been to protect human life by saving babies from abortion and they still remain the only maternity homes in the two Florida counties they serve. Their mission is only possible by helping the mothers of those babies and the best way to do that is by the transforming love and power of Jesus Christ. In fact, it's the only way.

One young woman, 21 years old, couldn't believe SOLVE was such a nice place and wanted to know "what's in it for you?" Abandoned by her family, she could not comprehend why strangers would offer help when no one else would. The why and the how is God.

Helen knew it from the very beginning when she heard his voice during the presentation at her church: "Do something. They're killing my babies." Many times she might have been tempted to quit; hers was not an easy vocation. But knowing that God had entrusted her with an important task she persevered, asking him every morning, "What are we going to do today?" She knew without a doubt that he kept it going and she was his instrument.

As she and Roland advanced in years, they never stopped helping with SOLVE. Just a month before he passed away in

2010 at the age of 91, Roland drove up to the parish center of Sts. Peter and Paul the Apostles Catholic Church and with his characteristic smile and twinkle in his eyes, dropped off a big load of donations for the annual rummage sale to benefit the organization he and his wife had founded. Their faithfulness would be admirable in someone being paid to do the work. That they were always volunteers was simply an astounding and miraculous sign of the power of saying yes to the Lord.

Donna knows, too, that her strength comes from God. "God's favor has been upon me because there is no way I could have taken on this role without him," she said. "God has brought us through many struggles, and the key word is through! Being part of SOLVE is a great calling because it is the difference between life and death; a physical life for the baby and a spiritual life for the mother," said the woman who had been there at the first breath of life and the last breath before eternity.

SOLVE offers girls the chance to continue their education, get job training and lots of other classes which are certainly important, but it is the love of Jesus Christ which opens their heart to meaningful changes. "Life comes to us in staggering contrast; there is goodness and love, laughter and beauty. Right alongside there is heartbreak, trial and affliction," said Donna. "Most of our residents come with shattered, broken, bruised lives — they have lost direction and hope."

Through the guidance and encouraging words from house managers and staff, without judgment or criticism, they begin to see that God's unfailing love is meant for them, too. They begin to have hope for a better life, understanding the truth of Jeremiah 29:11: *For I know the plans I have for you, declares the Lord, plans to prosper you and not to harm you, plans to give you hope and a future.* "We believe in the promises of God and stand amazed at the miracles which continue to happen at SOLVE," said Donna.

In the spring of 2013, after 14 years as the Executive Director and just a month after the 1,000th baby was born to a SOLVE resident, the beloved Miss Donna retired to spend more time with her own family, which now included seven young grandchildren. The Board chose Peggy to take over the reins of SOLVE. Stepping into the shoes of such a successful and charismatic leader is never easy, and it placed a big burden squarely on Peggy's shoulders. Despite knowing that God would direct her, Peggy feared the ship would sink on her watch. She fretted over decisions. She stressed. She worried. She just knew that she would be blamed if anything bad happened.

Then, one night, God whispered into the stillness of Peggy's heart. "He reassured me that SOLVE is his, and I am just his instrument right now," she said. "All I have to do is come to work each day and do my best and he will do the rest." Filled with God's grace, Peggy's confidence soared and she now knows without a doubt that she is right where she belongs. No, she is not Donna. But she, too, has been called by God to lead SOLVE and she will do it with his help, just as Donna and Helen had done before her. Surely Helen, who passed away in 2011, must be nudging the angels with a grin, "Will you look at that. He's done it again. He's brought the right person at the right time."

He continues to write the SOLVE story through each and every girl who says yes to life and through the tireless volunteers and dedicated staff who say yes as an ordinary housewife did more than 37 years ago. And so the staff gathers together every morning to begin the day with prayer, imploring God to drench their speech, their actions and their lives with his Holy Spirit, for it is only in Christ and through Christ that SOLVE continues. Knowing SOLVE is God's ministry, they can push forward as there is still so much work to be done.

"All thanksgiving and glory goes to Him who has allowed us to save His children."

Acknowledgements

I thank God for giving me the great privilege of compiling the history of SOLVE Maternity Homes and inspiring me to write this book. It has taken me about seven years from the time I wrote the first story, "Miss Donna Come Quick," to the time of publishing. Of course, during much of that time I was not actively writing the book because, well, writing a book is hard work! But I do thank my dear friend Joelise Jandric whom God used at the right moment to remind me when I was discouraged that I was indeed called to write this story and to "Get to work!" Those were the words I needed to hear.

I would have written none of these pages if it weren't for another dear friend, Jan Schuster, who invited me to join the SOLVE Board of Directors on a seemingly normal day in 2001, setting me on an incredible adventure of blessings I never expected.

The story of SOLVE Maternity Homes, spanning nearly four decades now, is filled with many more people than those mentioned in these pages and I acknowledge their tremendous contributions. So many people helped in so many ways, sometimes for years, giving of their time, talent and treasure. I wish I could have included more of them. They are certainly remembered for what they have done for "the least of these" and yes, this is their story, too.

My deepest gratitude to Helen Cadoret, the founder of SOLVE, for trusting me with her memories and with her precious scrapbook and for having the faith and courage to say yes to the Lord and never giving up. She remains a great inspiration to me and left a legacy that will impact many generations into the future.

Thank you, Donna Vellenga for all you did for so many years for the moms and babies of SOLVE and for your servant leadership. You are a passionate example of what it means to live for Christ and I treasure our friendship and your Christian witness.

I am indebted to all of the staff, volunteers and mothers who shared their stories with me.

To my mother, Olga J. Berg, who nurtured my love of reading and writing and encouraged me in the publication of this book. Thank you for being my Junior Great Books teacher in 7th grade!

I am grateful to Nancy Thibault, for introducing me to the wonderful people of Peppertree Press and for sharing in my excitement at the prospect of publication.

My prayer is that this book will inspire every reader with the knowledge that God works in our lives through other people, that his love and help is ever present, and that he does indeed have a plan for each of us, from the moment of our conception until we draw our final breath. It is also my fervent hope that readers will come to understand that, as I heard Donna say so many times over the years, "The baby is not the problem."

"You knit me in my mother's womb…
Wonderful are your works"
PSALM 139: 13-14

For more information about SOLVE,
visit
www.manasotasolve.org

Photo Gallery

*Helen and Roland married in 1945,
three months after he returned from the war*

Photo Gallery

Helen took many of the hotline calls herself

Photo Gallery

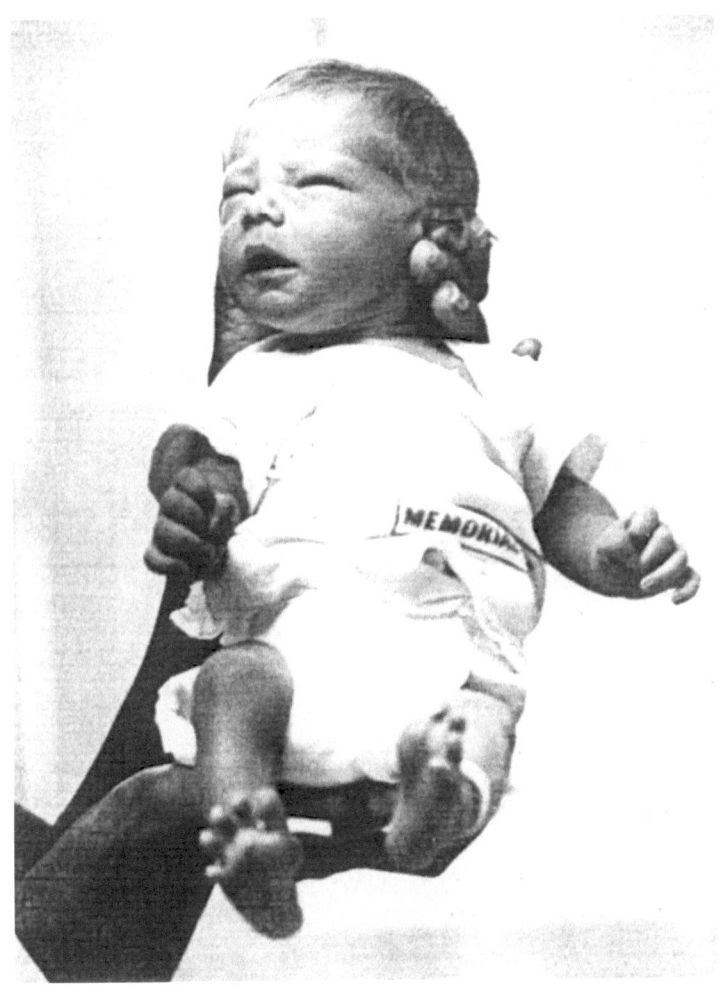

SOLVE's first baby, a boy, born September 1, 1976

Photo Gallery

The duplex, SOLVE's first maternity home 1977

SOLVE purchased this charming home in 1982

Photo Gallery

SOLVE office building opened in November 1984

Lunch break for volunteer workers in the SOLVE House 1989

Photo Gallery

Helen with the first twins born to a SOLVE resident 1994

Photo Gallery

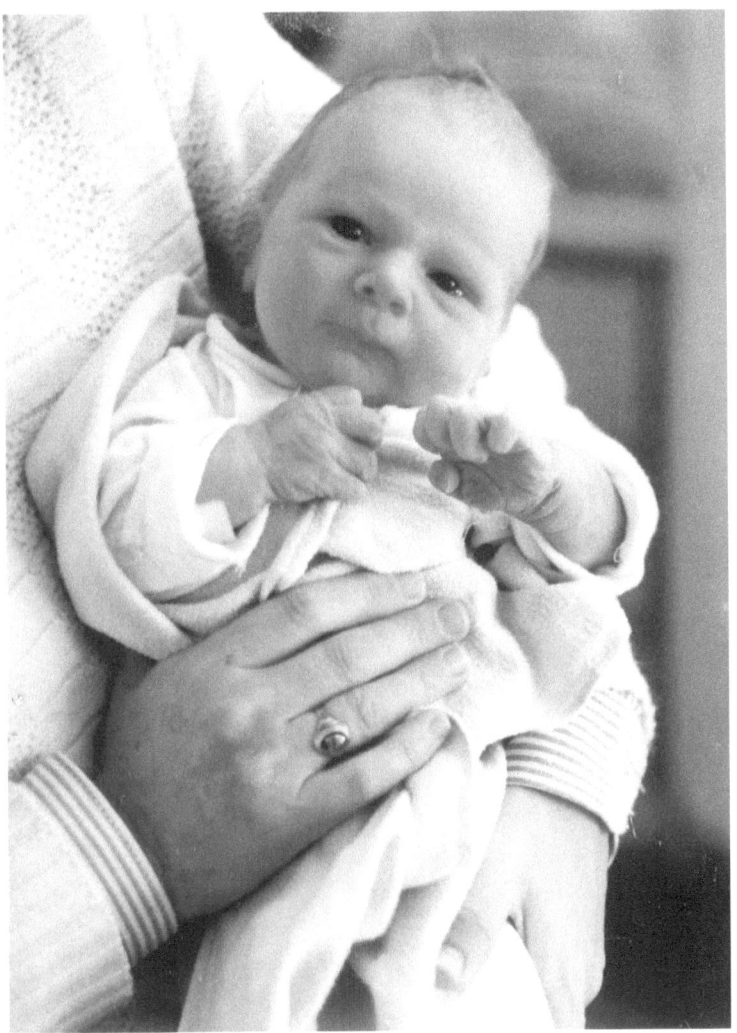

Beautiful boy 1988

Photo Gallery

The Cadorets - still going strong after 20 years

Sister Gloria, standing left, with girls at dinner, 1994

Photo Gallery

House mother Reina Avalos with a resident and her baby, 2000

Curt Vellenga, Donna's husband, with a SOLVE baby, 2001

Photo Gallery

Donna captures the moment when clearing land for SOLVE 2 begins May 2003

Helen and Roland break ground while Donna and building chairman Russ Dozeman look on June 1, 2002

Photo Gallery

Helen A. Cadoret, founder of SOLVE, 2003

Helen and Reina Avalos, Donna's assistant, accept a donation from Knights of Columbus members Ron Foley, left, and Mike Dyer June 19, 2003

Photo Gallery

Donna at a fundraiser with sketch of proposed House #2 at her left September 2003

SOLVE House 2 was completed in March of 2004

Photo Gallery

SOLVE's founder and Executive Director celebrate Open House at SOLVE 2 March 14, 2004

Photo Gallery

Peggy Kerwin was named Executive Director of SOLVE in March of 2013